Introduction to
Modern Existentialism

Randy Manning

Introduction to Modern Existentialism

ERNST BREISACH

GROVE PRESS, INC. NEW YORK

Tenth printing

Library of Congress Catalog Card Number: 61–11779

Manufactured in the United States of America

Advice and encouragement came to me from Dr. Abbie Copps, Olivet College, Dr. Robert Friedmann, Western Michigan University, and my wife Herma. I am deeply indebted to them for their unselfish help.

E.B.

Contents

I. Existentialism and the American Malaise

We do not know how or when it happened. But suddenly the high noon of joyful expectation has left us. The mood of crisis has come as an unwanted but permanent guest. And there is no escape. Wherever we turn somebody hurls the word crisis at us, whether it be in newspapers, in books, in sermons or in discussions. No wonder there has begun a fervent, often frenzied, soul-searching for the causes of this malaise.

The resulting diagnoses have varied. The "technicians" have maintained that the predicament of modern man is the result of one particular, simple-to-grasp problem, such as the dwindling thickness of the topsoil, the population explosion, the need for a better world organization, "bringing ethics into line" with our advanced technology, etc., etc. At heart they are all engineers, convinced that a quick repair is all that is needed. The "traditionalists" ascribe the malaise of contemporary Western man to his straying away from time-honored and well-proven ways. The ready answer to our malaise, they say, lies in readopting the religious or the political ideas of past centuries. Others have put the blame for our predicament on what they consider the stifling routine of modern life and have suggested nonconformity as the cure. The "prophets of doom," finally, have all along asserted that the mood of crisis shows our culture to be in its declining phase. They have labeled every attempt at rescue as well-meaning but futile.

After a brief period of fascination all of these diagnoses and prescriptions begin to pall and doubts arise about the analyses of both the black pessimists and the cheerful optimists alike.

This disenchantment, in turn, has become a strong incentive to explore existentialism and its suggestions. How exactly the ideas of the existentialists fit into our soul-searching has been the subject of lively dispute on the American intellectual scene. Negative judgments about existentialism have been loudly voiced. These criticisms have ranged from the belittling of existentialism as just another version of nonconformity or a requiem to a dying European culture to the biting condemnation of existentialism as a strange mixture of "Parisian pornography and Teutonic brooding." On the other hand, existentialism has also acquired serious and fervent adherents. One can safely say, however, that the most common American reaction to existentialism has been a widespread bewilderment.

Both opponents and advocates have had their share in bringing about this bewilderment. But one of its more fundamental causes has been the philosophy of existentialism itself with its peculiar structure. Nobody has yet or will ever put down "the" tenets of existentialism in a systematic work of so many volumes, nor will there at any time appear an "Existentialist Manifesto" which would neatly spell out easy-to-grasp maxims. Even the word existentialism itself must be used with great caution, since it refers not to a rigid set of propositions but rather to a number of themes which recur in the works of existentialist writers, themes which resemble neither prescriptions for cure-alls nor ready-made explanations of all that puzzles man. Instead they dwell on the eternal tensions present in the human condition and shared by men of all ages.

What are some of these themes? One which has fascinated all existentialists equally is the fervent appeal to every person to recognize that the human life is an adventure. For some of the existentialists this has implied the venture to live in constant awareness of the mystery of human existence; for others it has been the call to create meaning in an otherwise meaningless world. In both cases, however, existentialists have asked for a life in which man continuously questions his purpose and accepts responsibility for his actions, one which truly reflects man's special position in this world. To such a life, gripped totally by the drama of human existence, existentialists refer when they speak of an authentic existence, even though they differ widely in their interpretations of it.

In this view of the human life lies the root of another theme of existentialist thought: the hostility to closed systems, secular or religious, which pretend to be exact mirrors of what the world is all about. We shall see that existentialists battle against such systems for many reasons. They have shown through philosophical analysis the impossibility of man's building a universally valid system of thought which will enable him to "view" truth from the outside like any other object. They have also feared the intolerance which such systems breed when they seduce people into imagining themselves in possession of absolute truth. And even if fanaticism should be avoided, another danger of which existentialists have shown no less dread is the consequent lack of interest in further questioning one's life: an attitude, as Martin Buber puts it, of satisfaction that one has built a house in which one can live comfortably from now on, and from which one can look out upon the world with curiosity but without serious concern. Life instead of being an adventure turns into a "secondhand" life, the more so since most people do not create their own systems but merely accept them. Even the creators of systems all too often just put them together without ever involving their personalities wholeheartedly in them. This specter of a "secondhand" life in which the immediacy of human experience is dulled by routine living with routine explanations or even lost in it is what is meant by another recurrent existentialist phrase, man's estrangement from what he can be. Leo Tolstoy, not ordinarily counted among the existentialists, has nevertheless written a deeply moving short novel which sheds additional light on this somewhat strange term, and on other existentialist themes. Ivan Ilyich, the tragic hero of *The Death of Ivan Ilyich*, had been a shining example of a Russian officer, husband, father, and member of the Russian upper class of unflinching conformity. Then he suddenly becomes fatally ill, and his routine world collapses. Now he realizes that he has led a life of acted roles similar to those of countless other indistinguishable routine lives but not that of the unique Ivan Ilyich. In his last few days, filled with anguish and despair and, finally, with triumph, he becomes truly himself.

Admittedly, so brief a glimpse of some of the major themes of existentialist philosophy—life as an adventure, hostility against systems, authentic existence, and man's estrangement from his true self—adds still more questions to those one already has. But it does reveal the tenor of this philosophy. Existentialism emerges as a philosophy which demands a radical, personal, and never-ceasing questioning of the purpose of human life, destined "to keep one's soul on tiptoe, on the tiptoe of expectation";[1] a questioning which is demanded in the interest of what can justifiably be called the central existentialist concern, the actually existing individual. In its defense Kierkegaard had already said: "Each age has its own characteristic depravity. Ours is perhaps not pleasure and indulgence or sensuality, but rather a dissolute pantheistic contempt for the individual man."[2] And while other existentialists have not shared Kierkegaard's reasons for uttering these words they have all shared the anxiety which provoked them.

The contemporary malaise finds here a diagnostician who represents a fervent revolt in favor of the individual man which had its beginning in the early nineteenth century and, thus, cannot be called a passing fashion. Still, at this point, some doubts return. The eighteenth-century enlightened thinker, the romantic, the anarchist, and a host of others all have revolted in favor of the individual man. The skeptics have always asserted that man can find for his problems no ultimate answer which would be beyond challenge. Scores of modern thinkers, following the lead of Ortega y Gasset's *The*

Revolt of the Masses, have expressed their misgivings about the so-called mass society. Others have summoned us to a nostalgic journey back into what they consider to have been the golden days of individualism. Superficial similarities make it only too easy to group existentialism with some of these and to deny this philosophy its own clear identity. Consequently the value of existentialism both as a diagnosis of the contemporary malaise and as a part of perennial philosophy will hinge upon the answer to two questions: Does existentialism surpass in scope and in depth the other diagnoses of our predicament and previous revolts in favor of the individual man? And does it do this to a significant enough degree as to bring us closer to the quick of life?

II. Existentialism Prepared

Our time has formed the habit of referring to itself as the "Age of Crisis" or "Age of Anxiety." By a similar characterizing the era between 1815 and 1914 would have to be labeled the "Age of Confidence." This is accurate even despite ample misery and conflicts, the shouts and shots of revolutions and wars, and the radically shifting political borders. All of this happened without destroying the confidence that the final triumph over man's perennial problems was near and the mystery of human life itself would soon have to yield to man's inquiring mind.

Such an age could not but treat existentialist thinkers as outsiders and eccentrics: those men who, much as they may have differed in other respects, lived in a common awareness that the "human problem" had not been solved at all, and that all of the achievements hailed by the many were fraught with dangers for man. Dangers which lurked in taking superficial harmony and welfare for final solutions, scientific theories for ultimate truth, "isms" for new types of faith with utopian rewards and, most serious of all, in losing sight of the unique and living individual. One cannot really blame the contemporaries of these critical thinkers for regarding them with a mixture of incomprehension and irritation. Who, for example, amidst a tranquil Danish society which seemed to reconcile Church, State, and individual in a perfect union, could be so ridiculous as to speak of such things as fear, trembling, suffering, anxiety, and despair as part of the religious endeavor of man? Why should a Kierkegaard attack the society, the thought and, above all, the Church in and with which he lived? And then

Nietzsche. Why could he not join, with his splendid style, the panegyrists of the age of comfort and happiness? Why did he have to say "those unpleasant things"? And should not the others like Dostoevski and the modern artists swell the ranks of those who march confidently toward the promised fulfillment of all human dreams? Those who were the trail blazers of existentialism in the nineteenth century were lonesome figures. Their demand for a new approach to man's life, for the abandonment of the illusion that man had found "the" answer, and for the critical review of the blessings of the nineteenth-century society, science, and technology in the name of man himself went unheard. The true revolutionaries of that century were ignored by a people who suddenly woke up only when the cannons of the First World War dispelled their pleasant dreams.

A. The Revolt of the "Single One" —Sören Kierkegaard

1. THE CHALLENGE—HEGEL'S GRAND SYSTEM AND DANISH RELIGIOUS ROUTINE

From the time the last statesman left the Congress of Vienna, its dancing and negotiating ended, to the first shots of the revolutions of the year 1848, a sense of sheltered tranquility pervaded continental Europe. Man's restless quest for the ideal form of life, so explosively exhibited in the acts and ideals of the French Revolution, seemed suspended. Paternalistic monarchies watched over what they considered the well-being of their realms. The traditional religiosity was understood and accepted as religion. Tradition ruled supreme, undaunted by the first rumblings of socialism and nationalism. Man seemed finally at rest and his life firmly integrated into a meaningful whole.

To re-create now this mood of quiet and stability is well-nigh impossible. But that age left its lasting monument in Hegel's philosophical system: so towering a monument that much of later Western thought was an elaboration on either a "yes" or a "no" to Hegel. One of the "no's," passionately spoken and heartily ignored, comes from Sören Kierkegaard, the early protagonist of modern existentialism.

Whatever the Hegelian system may lack, it most certainly is not grandeur. Within it every human experience finds its meaningful place and every perplexing phenomenon its smooth explanation. It is one of those all-embracing systems in which the wonders of the comos are reflected in the mirror of total comprehension.

At the core of this grandiose system is the view of history as a single process with one beginning, one development, and one end. History is the world spirit unfolding, evolving from its entanglement in a not-so-spiritual world to its eventual self-realization in purity. Then the universally valid will triumph over the contingencies of the merely particular. In this process each historical stage fulfills its task, each culture makes its contribution, and each idea presents one particular although imperfect image of the world spirit. Nothing is left to chance. Chaos has disappeared from the world. What is is reasonable. Destructive forces are only seemingly harmful. In reality they are midwives of the new. The antithesis (the opposite) turns against the thesis (that which is) not out of malice, hatred, or conviction, but only to facilitate the better solution, the synthesis (the new stage).

Those who have said their "no" to Hegel have usually done so because they disliked one or more particular features of his system. Even such a vehement critic as Marx stays within the Hegelian system, although he wants to put it on "its feet"; that is, in direct opposition to Hegel he lets the economic conditions determine man's ideas. On the contrary the more radical "no" of Kierkegaard is provoked, not by a particular feature of the Hegelian system, but by its very image of man and the world.

A strange thing happens to man in the Hegelian system. Hegel attempts to elevate man to a privileged position by clearly distinguishing him from the objects of nature. Of the latter the most that can be said is that they are present at a given place at a given time. Man, on the other hand, constitutes a unity in himself, being conscious of himself. Thus he participates in the stratum of the spirit. For a moment man seems to be endowed with a special position in the world. But this promise is never redeemed in the Hegelian system.

First, pure thought and its development represent the only genuine reality. Everything else is reflection. Accordingly the man of flesh and blood with his feelings, fears, sorrows, joys, loves, and hates has no room in it.

Second, the grand design of world history reduces the place of the individual's existence and actions to that of a grain of sand in forming a desert. While the grain of sand certainly makes a contribution, it hardly has decisive importance. Even the great men of history do what they do only under the inducement of the inevitable process of the unfolding world spirit. They are tricked into doing it by a sly process. Man has become the agent of an all-powerful process. The world is the stage, history the drama, man the actor, and the self-realization of the spirit its final denouement.

And the world? It is emptied of all that is strange, startling, and even frightening in it. Man knows the master plan, and all the human problems immediately become of minor proportions. Closely connected with this is the vanishing of all true antagonisms from the world scene. In Hegel's concept of dialectical development each thesis and its antithesis merge into the higher unit of a synthesis. Man's conflicts are eventually superficial since they are always dissolved in the ensuing development. Man's decisions are of more importance as contributions to the on-going process than for himself. The full-blooded reality of life has been swallowed up by the world spirit which alone has actual reality. If all of this had been only the work of a philosopher whose influence had been confined to other philosophers, as is true in so many cases, Kierkegaard would hardly have protested against it so violently. But Hegel was the great symbol and schoolmaster of his time. No field of human endeavor escaped his influence. The idea of the dialectic which eleminates all true antagonisms led to a fascination with the "general" development, the "grand" view, and the consolation that even the worst catastrophes of this world had their meaningful place. This spirit of dialectical harmony, with its total loss of the really deciding individual, of risk, and of true freedom, even penetrated deeply into nineteenth-century Christianity. It was here that Hegel's philosophy challenged Kierkegaard most intimately. Out of their collision was born the "knight of faith," the man of the either/or, in short the existential Christian.

2. THE CALL FOR THE EXISTENTIAL CHRISTIAN

A life of passionate concern. The setting was an inconspicuous one for any revolution, intellectual or political. After the rather turbulent Napoleonic period, the Copenhagen of the nineteenth century displayed all the tranquility of a sheltered life. Away from the mainstream of history, it felt secure under the protection of a paternalistic monarchy and content with the reassuring guidance of the Established Church. Man's passions appeared to be well channeled and his fundamental problems reduced to manageable proportions. The man destined eventually to disturb this serene calm was in the early 1830's not too conspicuous either. True, Sören Kierkegaard seemed to be a brilliant young man. And like his fellow students he loved gaiety and diversion and sought them in theaters, cafés, and the company of women. But in him the smooth surface hid disturbing undercurrents. Sometimes his malaise reached such proportions that he felt a strong urge to commit suicide. Much of his early *Weltschmerz* can be attributed to a quite unusual childhood and adolescence. During these years the main influence came from Sören's father. Michael Pedersen Kierkegaard, through good fortune, had been able to leave the lonely heath of West Jutland, where he tended sheep, and come to Copenhagen. There he succeeded well in his business ventures, so well indeed that in his early forties he retired from business to devote all his time to contemplation of life, the world, and God. Deeply disturbed by some events in his earlier life, the elder Kierkegaard all too often brooded more than he contemplated. Hungry, cold, and lonesome in the often inhospitable heath of West Jutland, while very young and tending sheep, he had cursed God for the kind of life he had to live. Soon afterward fortune had smiled on him and made him a well-to-do man. Then during the sickness and after the death of his first wife he had entertained relations with one of his maidservants, who soon became the second Mrs. Kierkegaard. Even after this—as he interpreted it—second great guilt, his successes continued. Was this to be taken as a sign of God's infinite mercy or as a case of divine irony? In asking himself this question over and over, Michael Pedersen found himself returning again and again to the problem of the relationship between God and man.

When Sören grew up, a frail child with a somewhat hunched back and uneven legs, he soon became the favorite, although mostly receptive, confidant of his father. The grave doubts and dark despairs of adulthood were poured into the mind of an adolescent. It is not surprising therefore that the student Sören Kierkegaard with all his outward brilliance and gaiety was closer to the deepest human concerns than his associates.

The year 1837 brings the first of the crucial events in Sören Kierkegaard's life. At first it seems only too common. He met a young girl, Regina Olsen, and fell deeply in love with her. An engagement followed in due time. But then the lives of the two lovers became filled with agonizing and tortured moments. Their source always lay in Sören, who as soon as he had become engaged was beset by an onslaught of deeply troubling doubts. In many of his later writings Kierkegaard analyzed his situation at that time and tried to jutify his breaking the engagement in August, 1841. Whatever the reasons he gives, two main characteristics of Kierkegaard's personality and thought become clearly visible here. First, marriage, which others view lightly as being a ritual followed by a somewhat conventionally restricted life, Kierkegaard finds a challenge of major proportions. He is overwhelmed by the responsibilities marriage implies. Second, his conviction that isolation alone guarantees the integrity of a human life. These characteristics are reflected in many of the questions he asked himself. Does marriage mean just a change of routine, or is not one's whole life at stake? Is the promise of eternal faithfulness and love not a very audacious thing to make, a challenge almost too severe for a human being? How can two persons lead a life of total unity without losing their identities?

Many critics have asserted that this whole questioning in itself shows the morbidity of Kierkegaard's mind. Although he certainly magnified the problems, and saw primarily the limiting qualities of marriage for the human person, a critic would have some difficulty in showing that the unquestioned acceptance of ritual and custom is the healthier alternative. This is especially true if one knows that underlying all of his reasons was the spirit of sacrifice. Kierkegaard could not reconcile his ideal of a religious person with marriage, which necessarily introduces other obligations into man's life. Kierkegaard in a sense had already become the existential thinker for whom he called later on. And soon he had his first experience of being a lonely individual when for a good while he was ostracized by practically everybody for his break with Regina.

Some years of study in Berlin followed, filled with thinking of Regina, writing, and listening to the lectures of the famous philosopher F. W. J. Schelling. Already at this time the antagonism to Hegel, which later on becomes so important in his work, began to emerge. These years were also his last quiet ones. Soon Kierkegaard entered the public arena in a merciless journalistic fight. Characteristically it was brought about by Kierkegaard himself when he deliberately broke with the satirical magazine, *The Corsair*, although it had always been sympathetic to him. Kierkegaard thought that he owed it to his integrity to get rid of the support of the magazine, whose political outlook he did not share. The price of this uncompromising attitude was a period of ridicule during which even the boys in the street shouted the witticisms of *The Corsair* at him. He again became lonely, somewhat bitter, and a staunch enemy of all journalism. His latent conception of the crowd as inimical to the true human life and his certainly overemphasized view of the virtue of the isolated individual, were further strengthened. In the end Kierkegaard won, since Meir A. Goldschmidt, the owner of *The Corsair* and at heart always sympathetic to Kierkegaard, dropped the magazine in the year 1846, in the middle of the fight.

It shows Kierkegaard's strength that during this time of extreme hardship he prepared a still more awesome fight. The target of his new attack was to be nothing less than the Established Church of Denmark. During the years from 1847 to 1851 his writings were concerned with his views on Christianity. He still worked under pseudonyms, partially because he had doubts about his worthiness, partially out of respect for Bishop Mynster. The latter had been an intimate friend of Michael Kierkegaard and always remained an object of respect for the son. Only after Mynster had died in January, 1854 did Kierkegaard openly attack the Established Church, and the kind of Christianity it stood for. Now he wrote articles that were direct and easy to grasp. The result was turmoil, tribulations suffered from a hostile public, but also some support. Kierkegaard's health deteriorated. His last publication is dated May 24, 1855. Then he became silent. After a physical breakdown and a short period of hospitalization Kierkegaard died on November 11, 1855. His death thus resembles that of a shooting star—a period of especially bright light just before the final extinction.

One outstanding characteristic of Kierkegaard's work every reader will get to know very early—his preference for indirect communication. Highly developed by Kierkegaard, indirect communication pushes the unsuspecting reader to a point where he no longer merely reads a book but is himself undergoing experiences. The special affinity of this type of communication to the existentialist endeavor must even at this point be obvious.

The fundamental relation—God : Man. Kierkegaard's work, futhermore, does not add up to a well-ordered system, a fact which is understandable if one realizes the aim of Kierkegaard's philosophizing. He does not, for example, deal with those questions which so fascinate the natural scientists. Consequently Kierkegaard's thought, since it lacks a philosophy of nature, has often been characterized as anthropocentric. This is, to say the least, incorrect. The central problem of Kierkegaard's philosophy embraces both God and man. The relationship between these two beings poses the real all-important question for Kierkegaard. That God exists, even that he must be understood in Christian terms, is never doubted. But one can hardly say that Kierkegaard therefore fits smoothly into the Christian thought of his period. God, for Kierkegaard, is synonymous with the principle of eternity, infinity, and the absolute. Man was created in the image of God. In his freedom he has estranged himself from God. Man above all is a finite and particular being. Between him and God there is therefore an impassable gulf. The infinite absolute and the finite particular cannot be "united" in any way. Whether one tries as a mystic to leap over this gulf in moments of ecstasy, or hopes to bridge it by building theological or philosophical systems subsuming God and man alike in their paragraphs, the result will be total failure. As an example, Kierkegaard points to Hegel, whose attempts to integrate God, man, and religion in general into a universal system led to the loss of real importance of all of them.

If then the enormous gulf between God and man is accepted as a basic fact, what does it mean to live as a Christian? Kierkegaard approaches this question empirically, i.e. he not merely speculates but uses the total experience of his life to bring forth an answer. Certain philosophers would probably object to the use of the word "empirically" in this sense. However, if one does not interpret the term in the narrow way of sensuous observation, case-experimentation, and measurement, its use in this connection is justified. The more so since Kierkegaard's life and thought actually represent one long and searching experiment in the relationship between man and God. In such an experiment man is not an outside observer but stands in the very core of the experiment himself. Very soon the central importance of this fusing of thought and life for all of existentialism will become even clearer.

Man's modes of existence. Kierkegaard then proceeds in a logically quite consistent way to trace through the stages of his own life the answer to what it means to lead a Christian life. But in what some critics have pointed out to be a contradiction present in all of existentialism, he actually ascribes more than purely personal importance to the three stages of life he comes to distinguish: the aesthetic, the ethical, and the religious. Since the word stage somehow implies a rigid sequence, the term modes of living is actually preferable. Mode also indicates that a dominance of one way of life over the other is implied and not the exclusive presence of one.

The aesthetic mode of living shows man deeply involved in the world of immediacy. Like the child, the aesthete we all are at one time, he lives in the moment. He tries always to remain in the moment of pleasure and to forget all continuity and personal involvement in his life. The aesthete is essentially a driven man, even if he thinks he is pursuing a life of purpose. He is easily fascinated, but just as easily tires of everything. And in this pursuit of the sensuous and the sensual which in the last essence is a chasing after enjoyment, man is unable really to communicate because he is solely concerned with himself. Kierkegaard mentions a few famous examples of the aesthetic mode. Don Juan, whom he knew from Mozart's *Don Giovanni,* is one. Don Juan tries to fill his life with eroticism and fails. Faust—no doubt surprisingly to some readers—is another case in point. Although he already shows reflection, Faust never ventures into serious commitments, as, for example, religious ties. And finally there is Ahasuerus, the haunted Jew, who restlessly crisscrosses the world. He proves that the aesthetic mode knows its form of suffering too. But it is caused by the environment and not by a genuine inner struggle. The aesthete best known to modern man is probably the purely theoretical thinker, who finds his moments of excitement in his observing and theorizing, but who never seriously commits himself to anything.

The ethical mode sees man abandoning the attitude of the spectator and making commitments. He begins to wrestle with the concept of responsibility. Kierkegaard's own experience led him to discuss the ethical mode mainly in terms of marriage. Here a general code makes demands and man decides to live according to it. He decides but once, yet the consequences are life-long. Man with all his weaknesses takes it upon himself to commit himself unconditionally. It may seem strange to those who regard Kierkegaard as a Christian thinker that he considers marriage as purely ethical, lacking any religious dimension. The answer lies, of course, in Kierkegaard's insistence on the interpretation of religion as referring to man's lonely encounter with the totally "Other"—God. And thus man progressing to the third, the religious, mode of living leaves marriage behind with the ethical mode. Still the ethical mode is infinitely superior to the aesthetic one since it contains continuity and choice in freedom. It is, nevertheless, intrinsically deficient. Ethics is based on rational considerations. Universal demands are made in the form of codes which man accepts. He thus submits to abstractions and abstract bodies like societies. This submission, beneficial as it may be, leads at last to a dead end. The obstacle which prevents any real further progress in the ethical mode is the still-attempted self-sufficiency of man.

The way to break out of this containment is identical with the way to God. Only in the relationship to God does man as a total person confront authority. The experience of partial self-experience and involvement disappears now when not only the rational capacities of man but his whole personality is activated. Man finally recognizes himself as the unique individual he is. The insufficiency of all general rules for the individual and his unique situation becomes obvious. He experiences lonesomeness, risk or, as Kierkegaard puts it, fear and trembling.Kierkegaard uses the example of Abraham to illustrate the religious mode of living. Abraham puts his living personal relation to God above all moral laws when after a fierce struggle he decides to sacrifice his son. Here is the characteristic Kierkegaardian "leap" which projects man into a new mode of being. Abraham did not reason in syllogisms; a momentous decision gave his whole life a new direction. Not that man has now arrived once and for all at an ultimate goal and so to speak, possesses it. On the contrary he has immersed himself in a most exhausting struggle, the struggle to be worthy. He has accepted not a doctrine but a new way of life. Fulfillment is possible in it, not as an experience evoked suddenly and forever, but as a dynamic one.

The question as to what it means to be a Christian must of necessity be answered in the realm of the religious mode. The answer Kierkegaard gives seems at first sight fairly simple: to be a Christian means to strive after a Christian existence. This introduces the fateful and enormously complex term existence, which was destined to give a whole group of philosophers its name. To be sure they did not all endow the term existence with the same meaning. Kierkegaard, as one would expect, concerned himself exclusively with the problems surrounding a Christian existence.

Truth and authentic existence. First it may again be noted that the term existence as used by Kierkegaard and all existentialists is entirely divorced from its traditional connotation. According to the latter, existence refers to the mere fact that something is existent as opposed to essence which says what something intrinsically is. Each finite being participates in both of these categories. In God they are thought to be fused into one. In the nineteenth century, Hegel attempted to let the category "existence" vanish into the dynamics of the idea. A reality is left which merely acts out and manifests the process going on in the realm of essence. Actually man has become a shadow and life a shadow play. Kierkegaard's revolt against Hegel is against this, as he considered it, magic trick to let reality and especially the man of flesh and blood evaporate into pure thought. Kierkegaard thus set out to rescue the category existence from oblivion. But when he had rescued it, the term existence had acquired a totally new meaning.

During his years as a student, Kierkegaard had already criticized Hegel. Later he had heard Schelling attack Hegel in Berlin. Schelling classified Hegel's philosophy as a negative; that is, one which occupies itself with purely abstract terms and logical operations, and loses the connection with all that actually exists. Against it Schelling set positive philosophy, which has for its watchword reality. Actual being is its beginning and it proceeds from there to thought. Such a philosophy, of course, clearly recognizes the limitations of each logical system and constantly aims beyond systems into the endless vistas of reality. Kierkegaard had also read Trendelenburg's criticism of Hegel. Trendelenburg, too, pointed to the actual living man as the basis of all thought. He accuses Hegel, like all system-builders, of mistaking his concepts for either existing things or actually operating processes. Hegel, he said, thus demonstrated that the more sophisticated a system becomes the more it loses touch with reality, and becomes a graveyard of spontaneity and creativity. The actual act of existence, so full and rich, stubbornly refuses to be enclosed in even the best system. Kierkegaard continued this criticism by citing Socrates against Hegel. Socrates delighted in showing how little the man knows who supposedly knows everything. He would have smiled at the very suggestion that the fullness and infinite complexity of life could be pressed between the pages of x volumes of a systematic philosophy. Would man's existence not be emptied of all its immediacy and philosophy of its questions if all that matters has been answered neatly and finally in paragraphs? Is not God the only one for whom the actual world forms a system? Furthermore, man participates in the world of full reality, he is a part of it and his decisions and actions matter decisively. It is futile for him even to try to be nothing but a speculative observer.

Systems, which pretend to comprehend everything but actually are able to make fully understandable only their own abstractions and which pretend to start without presupposition but are always based on an act of interpretation, can never be expressions of truth. But what then is truth if not objective and systematic? It will be subjective and inward. The artificial separation of truth (as a certain body of knowledge "outside" myself) from my personality will be overcome in a complete fusion. Truth is personal. Consequently, it will carry new aspects. The first one will be the emphatic accent on its nature as an on-going process. Systems with their tight sets of statements claim finality for their findings. But Kierkegaardian truth is based on reflection, which by its very nature is bound to go on as long as man lives. This impossibility of a "closed truth" in the form of a final body of knowledge which offers itself for ready acceptance brings with it a second element, objective uncertainty, an element so important that Kierkegaard uses it as the very starting point of his definition of truth: "An objective uncertainty held fast in an appropriation-process of the most passionate inwardness is the truth, the highest truth attainable for an existing individual."[1] Truth is, thus, a state in which the person feels himself hanging from a precipice (objective uncertainty) and yet is filled with a passion for the infinite.

It is not surprising that Kierkegaard's definition of faith is practically identical with that of truth. In both cases the object of knowledge reaches into the very inwardness of personality. It concerns the fundamental cleavage between the infinite absolute and the finite being. For Kierkegaard this is actualy all "that" man can know and that matters. But to say this in these factual and plain terms deprives this supreme paradox of human life of most of its depth. Objective truth can be expressed directly because it admits to no secrets or paradoxes. Subjective truth does not lend itself to direct utterance, because it must be appropriated by an existent individual to become fully meaningful. While in objective truth the emphasis lies in "what is asserted," in subjective truth, the Kierkegaardian and existential truth, it lies in "how" the truth is appropriated. And with that, new light is shed on the term authentic existence itself. It refers in Kierkegaard to a certain way of life. One in which the link between truth and authenticity becomes visible. Accordingly, an existential thinker integrates into a unity his life in its fullness with his search for truth. He alone will find truth, whereas what Kierkegaard calls the objective thinker, disintegrated and purely speculative, will find little more than pale abstractions. "The thinker who can in all his thinking forget also to think that he is an existing individual will never explain life. He merely will attempt to cease to be a human being in order to become a book or an objective something which is possible only for a Münchhausen."[2]

Kierkegaard, who here lays another foundation for later existentialism, has been widely criticized for the alleged extreme subjectivity he introduced into the pursuit of truth. If this way of truth were accepted, the critics have agreed, anarchy would be the rule of the day in the intellectual field, since all commonly shared yardsticks would have disappeared. Whatever relevance this criticism may have for other thinkers in the existentialistic vein, it is not quite justified in the case of Kierkegaard. Nothing is further from Kierkegaard's mind than to advocate irresponsibility in human affairs. One of his reasons for reformation of the concept of truth was actually to combat the Hegelian de-emphasis of human responsibility. Human choice, decision, and action should carry real weight and not just be means or tricks of reason. He would bring against such critics the accusation that being an individual man has been abolished and every speculative philosopher confuses himself with humanity at large. It is this thinking of man in the abstract that results in real irresponsibility. A more pertinent objection to the criticism is that Kierkegaard dealt with truth in connection with the religious mode. This means that Kierkegaard was not just showing formally how to approach truth. This was not his general intention. Kierkegaard saw in the basic image of the world no longer a challenge to real questioning. In contrast to Nietzsche or Sartre, who base their works on the fundamental thesis that "God is dead," Kierkegaard starts from that expressed in the words "God lives." Man's fundamental relation is his relation to this infinite absolute which is forever separated from him. In the abandonment of himself to it he finds truth. Or as Kierkegaard says in the last sentence of *Either/Or*, "only the truth which edifies is truth for you."

Man's existence has its roots in God. His whole life is designed in a way which aims at ultimate harmony with God. But although this is so, one should beware of sentimentality. God, the infinite, the absolute, confronts man as the total "Other." Man knows he is a finite being. The more seriously he takes God, the more clearly he sees the gulf between God and himself. At the same time he realizes the impossibility of making God an object of knowledge and description. Herein lies the impact of the Kierkegaardian God, that he confronts man as person confronts person. He does not emerge as the highest possible of all abstractions after a long and elaborate climbing of the ladder of abstractions. This personal relationship necessarily introduces a great sense of immediacy and urgency into the life of man. It will be most clearly expressed in man's care for his eternal destiny. The average man considers physical death a frightening but still distant event. Others, like some philosophers, try to see death in some supposedly meaningful context. In doing so, according to Kierkegaard, they weaken its impact by finding some on for it or they deny any necessity for concern. But the idea of philosophy is mediation—Christianity's is aradox."[3] Christian thought is not to fill in the gap be-en beings and infinite absolute but to preserve it carefully as the great challenging truth.

Accordingly Kierkegaard demands that the religious mode be governed constantly by the awareness of another great paradox: that man, the finite being, can in the nearly negligible span of his lifetime make decisions for his eternal destiny. It is no wonder that the leap from the ethical to the religious mode is such an enormous event. Knowing the crucial importance of his life man experiences a deep anxiety. Aware of this awesome gift of freedom to decide rightly or wrongly, man will soon find his life resembling a whirlpool. Despair will never be far away. But only in this despair will there open up the possibility of becoming a Christian, or, to use the well-known term, of leading a Christian existence. Man has never been at a loss for means to escape such a strenuous life. Some, like Ivan Ilyich, choose to live as if the world of the everyday were the only thing which mattered. For a time this may be a successful way of avoiding inner disturbances. Or one can accept ready-made answers to prevent nagging basic questions from even arising. But the price paid is much too high. Man in his attempts to evade necessarily blocks himself permanently from the real source of his being.

Existential Christian versus Christendom. It is this problem of evasion on which Kierkegaard at the height of his life's work speaks out directly, a fact which accounts for the stormy last years of his life. But the aim of his attack is really not alone the Established Church of Denmark. It is what Kierkegaard calls Christendom or objective Christianity, a phenomenon much too widespread to be purely Danish. ". . . there is, of course, nothing which to its [the honesty of eternity] detective eye is so suspicious as are all fantastic entities: Christian states, Christian lands, a Christian people and (how marvelous!) a Christian world."[4] Here a Christian church might be added. All of these entities give the illusion that one is a Christian because one lives as one of their members. Kierkegaard, however, protests, "But gradually the human race came to itself and, shrewd as it is, it saw that to do away with Christianity by force was not practicable—'So let us do it by cunning' they said 'we are all Christians, and so Christianity is *eo ipso* abolished.' "[5] To the shocked surprise of many, Kierkegaard counted the Established Church of Denmark among the means of evasion; that is, it participates in the abolition of true Christianity.

A Christian existence—he held—has no necessary connection with being a member of a church, believing dogmas, accepting a creed, or dutifully attending church. The church cannot administer salvation through a salaried religious bureaucracy or the dispensing of sacraments. It is all too easy to be "Christian" in this way. At its best, the church can give guidance to the individual in his search for a personal relationship with God. This personal search, with its agony and bliss, must exist in man before the church can guide him. The central danger posed by Christendom is that man never has a chance truly to search, since what looks like satisfaction is offered to him even before any real religious quest can arise. This means to forget that the cross and what it symbolizes represents a challenge to the total person and should never be the fountainhead of doctrines. The church is at its worst when it identifies the acceptance of a predigested message with becoming a Christian. This complex of dogmas, rituals, and administrators of faith, which Kierkegaard calls objective Christianity (or Christendom), is nothing but the religious counterpart of secular, philosophical systems. Both pretend to give meaning to man's life and with it promise comfort and peace of mind. But the existential Christian—and there can never be an existential Christendom—ventures far beyond such evasive positions. He dares to risk his whole life in the decision to become a Christian. He also knows that he can never "be" but will always only "be becoming" a Christian by ever renewing his relationship with God and making it the decisive fact of his life. In this he has the invaluable guidance of Jesus Christ.

But even here man encounters a challenge to his whole person. Objectively to accept Christ's teachings as one accepts the correct results of a mathematical problem would be paganism. Nor are they as comforting as the crowd finds them to be. The many have even reinterpreted Christ's personality, "whereby again they have managed to transform Christ into a friend of tiny-tots *à la* Uncle Franz, or Godman or a charity school teacher."[6] (Uncle Franz and Godman were friendly figures in Danish children's book of Kierkegaard's time.) Christ's life, as seen by Kierkegaard, is the great "absurd," the great "scandal": the eternal God comes into existence in time as a particular man. God is born, lives, suffers, and dies in humility. All of this is so contrary to all human expectations that it is easier to take any kind of evasive position than wholeheartedly to accept it as the central fact of one's life. Truly a leap is required into a Christian existence. And for this again the Established Church is more an obstacle than a help. What challenge is there to become a Christian when everybody already calls himself a Christian? As Kierkegaard puts it, a "Christian of some sort" thinks that he has already done all that is needed. He has been baptized, confirmed, and married in church, and he frequents it from time to time on Sundays. After all "are you not a Dane, and does not the geography say that the Lutheran form of the Christian religion is the ruling religion in Denmark?"[7]

A little less naive but still an attempt of evasion is the reducing of the "absurd" to a set of readily acceptable propositions, which again blocks man's way to becoming an existential Christian. Christ wanted not admirers who memorize certain formulas but followers. The existential Christian faces a life of self-sacrifice. At every moment he must struggle to renew his contemporaneity with Christ. One who wants to derive comfort and peace of mind from his religion should shy away from this endeavor. A Christian existence is filled with suffering, with being offended by the radical demands of Christ, with repenting one's failures, and with "fear and trembling." There beckons no security but only everlasting risk. The reward, if it can be so called, is not a harmonious life but a life which fulfills itself in the light of its eternal dimensions. Such a life is always unique. No man, no process, and no trick can relieve man from the burden of going from the very bottom to the pinnacle of an authentic existence alone, suffering and struggling.

The Dane, like most people of the early nineteenth century, could not be other than startled by a person who once suggested that on his tombstone he would like to see only one inscription—the individual. Kierkegaard himself has probably best described the reaction of his contemporaries to his anguished call for a new Christian: "But if a man were to say quite simply and unassumingly that he was concerned for himself, lest perhaps he had no right to call himself a Christian, he would indeed not suffer persecution or be put to death, but he would be smothered in angry glances, and people would say: 'How tiresome to make such a fuss about nothing at all; why can't he behave like the rest of us, who are all Christians? It is just as it is with F.F., who refuses to wear a hat on his head like others, but insists on dressing differently.' "[8]

B. The Tragedy of a Prophet—
Friedrich Wilhelm Nietzsche

1. THE CHALLENGE: THE ERA OF HOPE AND CONFIDENCE

A deep silence followed Kierkegaard's life and work. It is not surprising that the religious aspect of his thought should have been ignored in a period which saw the rapid spread of secularization over all of Central and Western Europe. What is significant, however, is that no other element in Kierkegaard's work, especially the call for true individualism, was to become more influential. This the more so since the middle and the late nineteenth century saw the old authorities slowly but steadily weaken. The paternalistic monarchies and the traditional churches were confronted by serious challenges. Simultaneous with this process of disintegration appeared the first signs of the age of the common man, bringing with it the glorious promise—or better, the challenge—of individual freedom. Gradually, a degree of freedom became a rudimentary reality to at least the upper and middle strata of the societies.

But despite such a penetrating upheaval, the radical questioning concerning the meaning of man's life and the call for an authentic existence which had been the supreme themes for Kierkegaard and still remain so for existentialism, had hardly any impact on the thought of this period. Characteristically and fatefully, those who had become free chose all too often to use this freedom to dedicate their lives to a new authority. The new authorities were mainly the "isms" or systems of ideas which again seemed to afford a universal explanation of the world and thus to offer to man comfort and security. He could again rest assured in "the" knowledge of the structure and aim of the world. Furthermore, since the majority of these systems promised a necessarily better future, one could also look forward to it with great hopes and expectations. Moreover, under the "isms" all this could be achieved by merely changing the institutional organization of society. Kierkegaard had viewed the authentic life as one of continuous personal involvement. In most of the "isms" such a strenuous task could be avoided, since a single revolutionary or an evolutionary change of social institution would solve human problems forever.

Man, having hardly been liberated from age-old restrictions, fled from his newly won freedom. The Kierkegaardian freedom of the "single one" terrified him. He preferred to tie the destiny of his life to the more abstract development of mankind. This was easier, more comfortable, and a good deal more pleasant in its prospects for the future.

The way to do so was offered by the "isms" with their utopian and pseudo-religious flavor. Paradoxically, all of them had started out with a genuine concern for existing man, but somewhere along the way, out of this existential concern had developed systems of consolation.

Liberalism preserved essential parts of the original existential concern. As that "ism," which can be credited for practically all the individual freedom achieved by nineteenth-century Europeans, it always implied openness and tolerance for the most varied viewpoints. The liberal society never closed the door to a resumption of the searching and renewed creativity by its members. This, its greatest historical achievement, was marred but not destroyed when liberalism at certain periods grew into an ideology with its own full-fledged systematic image of the world. In this, its utopian version, it viewed society as a vast machine in which each man-particle was held in place by benevolent laws of nature. Provided no human interference occurred, human happiness would automatically result. Hence the principle of laissez faire, if allowed to rule supreme in all socio-economic matters, would assure progress to ever greater heights of happiness.

Nationalism mostly rejected the overly simple view of man as a particle in a mechanistically operating world. It thus penetrated somewhat deeper into the mystery of man, but again offered him a new escape from confronting himself with radically searching questions. Man could (and indeed did) submerge himself in the group, and by totally dedicating his life to it, again find a meaning to his life. It was a tragically one-sided meaning, but still it went beyond the shallow search for happiness.

In Marxism there is an especially wide gap between early probing into man's destiny and consequent systematic orthodoxy. The young Marx lived in the painful period of early industrial Europe when a whole layer of society was excluded from the benefits of man's inventiveness. The factory worker of this period became for Marx a symbol of how man could be estranged from his existence as a human being. He discovered that there could be disharmony in the midst of proclaimed progress and that a whole group of people could become mere tools rather than persons. But then Marx reverted to Hegel and incorporated the genuine problem and its suggested solution into a vast system. In it the idea or world spirit of Hegel is replaced by the forces of production. History is the story of groups who possess the tools of production exploiting those who do not (class struggle). Whatever phenomenon man encounters in his life is a mere superstructure above the fundamental and all-powerful economic forces. This is true for art, religion, education, social grouping, and other social and cultural phenomena. Each serves in its way at a given time a particular class of exploiters as a tool of exploitation. Only when the last class antagonism, that between capitalists and proletarians in the industrial society, will have been replaced by the establishment of the socialistic society, will man become fully man. This new organization of the socio-economic sphere will usher in the age of continuous happiness for all men. Marx, it is true, stressed the importance of the active commitment and dedication of each individual proletarian to the bringing about of the socialistic age. After all, it is a real struggle between human beings which is supposed to carry on world history. But the outcome of this struggle is never seriously in doubt. The system has a compelling logic of its own which leads straight to one end—the socialistic society. As in Hegel history achieves its own aim—man, however much he may fight is a mere actor, bad or good depending on the side he takes. No wonder then that Marxism in its systematic form, with its promise of happiness and certainty, became the source of hope, comfort, and security for the many.

The ideologies or "isms" were tightly interwoven with another current in the intellectual development of nineteenth-century Europe. In that century the sciences rose to a startling level of achievement and to a commensurably high prestige. Many, especially among the intellectuals, saw in them the possibility of building a view of the world which would be reliable if not compellingly certain. Was science not based on observation, experiments, quantifications, and other means undoubtedly of ultimate accuracy? Consequently the scientific cosmologies appear, some of them biologically, others mechanistically inspired. All of them integrate man tightly into nature and deny any fundamental breach between man and the realm of nature. In them the self-assertions of the individual become insignificant compared with the great forces of nature which dominate man and the processes which carry him along. The comfort which former generations had found in God was now offered by such abstractions as mankind, progress, and benevolent natural laws. Everything is so clear, so convincing, and so unassailable since it is supposedly "proven," that any wonder in man about himself becomes increasingly an anachronism.

Philosophy did not escape this spell of the sciences. For fear of becoming outdated it suspended the question which had lent vigor to philosophy since its origin: the question concerning man's position in the cosmos and his strange situation in being at the same time immersed in nature and lifted out of it. As a concession to the sciences, epistemology, the theory of how to know, became the main concern. Other philosophers wrote histories of philosophy much in the manner of chroniclers of a now finished endeavor of knowledge. Those who say "no" to this development are few and hardly ever in influential positions.

Confidence in the possibilities of science and the general development also left its mark on the Christian churches, especially when the "isms" and the new scientific cosmologies vehemently challenged the Christian world view. A variety of reactions appeared: Christian socialism, ethical Christianity (which dropped what it considered outdated metaphysical concepts), and numerous other compromises with one or the other contemporary force. As for Kierkegaard, however, his influence remained *nihil*. This *homo religiosus* with his themes of individual responsibility, freedom, and loneliness could have not been more ignored.

All of this leads to the great paradox of the nineteenth century. With all its concern for freedom and the individual, that age failed to see that the freedom and the dignity of the individual do not result spontaneously from the legal order, institutions, adherence to dogmas, or benevolent world processes. Too few were willing to recognize that freedom is a challenge, not a privilege and comfort, that the abysmal depths in human existence cannot be easily understood, and that it is much more fitting to put after the word "man" a question mark rather than an exclamation point.

Knowing this, one can easily sense the tragic clash which was destined to occur when still another thinker tried to voice a warning. With Kierkegaard dead and ignored, Friedrich W. Nietzsche, the "tragic philosopher," became the advocate of the necessary reappraisal.

2. THE CALL FOR "HIGHER MAN"

The revolt against the whole era of hope and enthusiasm came, as in Kierkegaard's case, from unexpected quarters. The family of Friedrich W. Nietzsche was what is called in German *gut bürgerlich* (solid bourgeois). With a long line of Lutheran ministers as ancestors, it showed a deep loyalty to the Church and the Hohenzollern dynasty. Friedrich's childhood was watched over by the four ladies of the Nietzsche household and later its intellectual side was entrusted to the famous monastery school at Schulpforta. Nietzsche spent his years as a university student at Bonn and Leipzig. It is perhaps an omen of unusual things to come that Nietzsche was called to teach classical philology at the University of Basel before he had completed his work for a doctorate in philosophy. This is a truly sensational happening in a European university. Hurriedly the University of Leipzig conferred the degree on Nietzsche before he left for Basel.

The Nietzsche of the pre-Basel and early Basel periods was primarily concerned with aesthetic problems. But even in his earliest work, *The Birth of Tragedy* (1872), he probed into spheres far beyond aesthetics and classical philology. By the very nature of his personality Nietzsche could not remain a mere classical philologist. While still a university student he had been deeply impressed by the philosophy of Arthur Schopenhauer (1788–1860). Schopenhauer's chief work, *Die Welt als Wille und Vorstellung* (*The World as Will and Idea*), which Nietzsche read when he was twenty-one had struck him like a revelation. His work and life showed the mark of Schopenhauer even after Nietzsche had later turned against him. There is in both the deep desire for truth without illusions, the willingness to admit disharmony in nature, and most significantly the central importance given to irrational will in the cosmos. According to Schopenhauer it is the will to live that makes man view the world as he does, finding order where there is none. Only the few who penetrate deeply enough into this world will, after destroying their illusions, arrive at the core of it all, the will to live. They will accept then a world without aim and harmony, the nonexistence of God and ethics marked by asceticism and compassion.

The Nietzsche of the early 1870's combined this influence with that of an intimate friend, Richard Wagner. For years Nietzsche hoped to find in Wagner the great innovator of European thought and art, and at no other time in his life did he find the happiness and tranquility of the period when Richard and Cosima Wagner were his friends living in nearby Triebschen. This made only the more bitter the much celebrated break with Wagner (1876) which resulted from a disillusionment naturally to be expected after such exalted hopes and from the suspicion that Wagner had surrendered to the very forces Nietzsche was determinedly fighting.

The break occurred at a time when Nietzsche was in general becoming weary of his position as a teacher of classical philology. He longed to have more time for his search for answers to the questions which so deeply concerned him and which by far transcended the philological realm. He was worn by the agony which accompanied so much of his search since his whole person was always deeply involved when he was thinking, questioning, or answering. This immediacy with which his intellectual endeavor affected his personal life is probably the first significant element linking Nietzsche with Kierkegaard and the later existentialists. After a short and welcome rest Nietzsche resumed teaching for another two years (1877–1879). Then he retired under the impact of a general physical breakdown from which he recovered by the year 1880. He continued writing for another nine years. After these years of exuberant creativity came the total and final collapse. From January, 1889 to his death in 1900 he was helpless and dependent on the care of his sister, Mrs. Elisabeth Förster-Nietzsche. Her care was beneficial to Nietzsche the man, but the price Nietzsche the scholar paid for it proved appalling. It was his sister who through outright deceit enabled chauvinists of all colors to quote Nietzsche as their proponent. This she accomplished through a unique system of "editing." And so Nietzsche was not only neglected for a long period after his death but, worse, he was misinterpreted for at least as long a time.

Plenty of critics have tried to depreciate Nietzsche's work because of his eventual nervous and mental collapse. The reasons for his collapse, whatever they were, are less important than the observation that there is nothing "abnormal" in his work (except the very last part done when he was really ill). The questions he asks are those put by many a keen observer of the world and man. He can be called "abnormal" only in his merciless probing of them to their very core and in the controversial but brilliant answers he has given. If this were to be classified as "abnormal," a goodly number of all philosophers and scholars in general would have to be pronounced "abnormal."

Nihilism and decadence. The most common approach to Nietzsche's work is chronological. Although this is admittedly the most fruitful way to analyze the work of so personal a philosopher as Nietzsche, it will not be used here. For our purpose, which after all aims not at a total but a selective presentation of Nietzsche's thought, another approach will be taken. What Nietzsche said I shall for my purpose differentiate into analysis and answer. Nietzsche himself at times distinguished his "no-saying" from his "yes-saying" work. The former, the analytical or critical part of his work, in which he mercilessly tried to point out and destroy what he considered the illusions of his time, should, however, not be viewed as purely negative. For Nietzsche disillusion was a necessity before a way could be cleared for new avenues of thought and life. Nowhere is this intention clearer than in his concern with nihilism. The latter actually stands at the very core of all his work. "What I relate is the history of the next two centuries. I describe what is coming, what no longer can come differently: the advent of nihilism. . . ."[9] He found the presence of nihilism at the end of all contemporary thought when it was analyzed. This was necessarily so, "because the values we have had hitherto thus draw their logical conclusions of our great values and ideas."[10]

Nietzsche preached the danger of nihilism to his contemporaries and he despaired at their lack of understanding. At times he even hoped for nihilism to reach its peak so that the doubters might at last recognize its presence. All of his ideals for man were purposely formed as a direct answer to nihilism. Concern with nihilism was also the basic proposition on which he built his work: God is dead. This proposition was not arrived at through long and intricate logical operations. Nietzsche was an empiricist of the Kierkegaard variety. The proposition that "God is dead" constituted for him an observation. It said nothing concerning whether God existed "in general." Such an argument would have been foreign to Nietzsche, who began—in good existentialist manner, indeed—with man as he experienced him outside and inside himself. And thus to say that "God is dead" means no more and no less than that he is dead for the majority of the Europeans of the time of Nietzsche. The Nietzschean analysis was aimed at showing that this crucial condition existed despite the most widespread conviction to the contrary. And in a striking parallel to Dostoevski, Nietzsche saw in the absence of God not an occasion for rejoicing but a terrifying challenge. "God is dead. God remains dead. And we have killed him. How shall we, the murderers of all murderers, comfort ourselves? What was holiest and most powerful of all that the world has yet owned has bled to death under our knives. Who will wipe this blood off us? What water is there for us to clean ourselves? What festival of atonement, what sacred games shall we have to invent? Is not the greatness of this deed too great for us? Must not we ourselves become gods simply to seem worthy of it?"[11]

With God, meaning and value systems depart from the world. A situation arises which threatens human dignity itself. But this also—as Nietzsche would confidently say—offers the first and supreme challenge for man to realize himself fully. Because of this he hopes man will become part of a "Higher History" than all history hitherto. The crucial point is that in order to overcome the onslaught of nihilism, man must go beyond his previous answers, which Nietzsche viewed as highways for the advent of nihilism. For far too long a time man had been clinging to answers which comforted him and alleviated his premonitions. These comfortable systems of thought, however, are not easily given up. And thus the advent of nihilism is quiet since it is well hidden behind a thick veil. In the belief that he is choosing means against nihilism, man embraces ideas which actually accelerate its coming. This leads to a condition which Nietzsche called decadence. At this point he shares with the existentialists disgust with what they would call unauthentic existence and he still terms lack of creativity.

Science—pioneer of nihilism. What then were Nietzsche's specific objections to the system of thought of his time? One battery of objections was directed against the alliance of science, humanism, and liberalism which he confronted in his time. The total scientific endeavor of Nietzsche's time was as deeply penetrated by the spirit and methods of the natural sciences as is ours, in fact much more uncritically so. Nietzsche never ceased to protest against a science of man which loses itself in the near worship of one method. Not a particular method but the passionate quest for knowledge characterizes scientific endeavor. But to Nietzsche, no less objectionable than worship of one method was the atomistic-mechanistic world view held by the sciences of his time. He argued that in the human sphere there are never the equal conditions which alone make situations comparable for experiments patterned after those in the natural sciences. Even the slightest differences are significant sources of error. Neither can exact measurements really be made since man is a part of a whole, the moving and therefore constantly changing world system. It is obvious how far ahead Nietzsche was in relation to scientists with strictly mechanistic notions. For him the scientific world view, patterned after the natural sciences, is only the world view of a special generation. Contrary to the generally held opinion its objectivity is no greater than that of previous views. Like all of them, it is based not on facts but on interpretations. Man knows no facts in the sense of statements which contain no elements of interpretation. Truth is always a subjective creation, knowledge always contains evaluation. The scientific world view is so widely accepted only because of its usefulness and not because it is the ultimate truth. It is based on presuppositions formulated and accepted by man. The world thus appears to be logical because we make it look logical.

However practical this viewpoint may be, it certainly offers no final explanation of the world. It does, however, do something else, something unexpected and unintended. It paves the way for nihilism. This is because of the tragic fact that the scientific world view destroys what it considers illusions but is totally unable to fill a human life with meaning. The very limitations it sets for itself—namely, not to affirm values but rather to describe existing ones—prevent the scientific world view from being genuinely constructive. All the sciences can do is analyze what man creates out of his passionate concern. They themselves are sterile. Even worse, new interpretations by the scientist are taken by many and blown up into a full-fledged world view with disastrous results. Nietzsche illustrated this point in his discussion of Darwinism. If man chooses to view himself as merely an animal involved in the struggle for existence, then he will become this animal, not because he factually is one but because he, so to speak, interprets himself into being one. Consequently human society will soon be full of the "brotherhoods of robbery and exploitation" which fit into such a world. Is there a better example of the existentialist contention that thought and life are intimately connected? Thought has consequences even if the thinker himself merely toys with his ideas. Another example of dangerous intellectual playing is offered by the humanist who first abolishes God and then shifts the functions of God to some such substitute as the goodness of man or benevolent natural laws. But with the vanishing of God who created man, "the" authority dies. No pseudo-gods can be substituted. The attempt to escape the impact of the death of God in the human heart through a scientific world view is destined to fail.

For liberalism with its political ideal of democracy Nietzsche has two criticisms, one of which even a person who views democracy as the most practical form of political life must heed and the other related to Nietzsche's own answer to nihilism. The first is directed against blind belief in inevitable progress, exaggerated expectations from democracy, and a too simple interpretation of man as good and liberty-loving. In short, Nietzsche, as any existentialist would do, warned against trying to transform the principles of equality, liberty, and fraternity into either a mechanical formula for achieving the best in everything or the creed of a pseudo-religion. The second criticism doubts the validity of the aim of democracy itself, which Nietzsche sees as the happiness of all or at least of the most. This ideal, as will be seen, conflicts with Nietzsche's vision of the creative few as the total meaning of history.

Nationalism as an attempt to give meaning to man's life receives equally severe criticism. Those who see in Nietzsche a chauvinistic German who worshiped pure power politics are fundamentally mistaken. Nietzsche spoke of himself often as the "good European." He wanted no part of that German nationalism which saw in political success an expression of cultural superiority. He held a purely negative view of the state of his time, especially the German *Reich* which had been founded in January, 1871. For him the state was the great corrupter of Christianity, and was on its way to develop into the great Leviathan. Soon the citizens would be on their knees before it and a dictator would be declared its high priest. Far from being a voluntary association of individuals for mutual protection, it was emerging more and more as the greatest drillmaster. It supported the uncreative trends in man, his laziness and fearfulness, by fostering and enforcing conformity. For Nietzsche the modern state represented no more than a fairly complicated herd, against which individuals would have to rise if they did not wish to be swallowed up. Nietzsche thus viewed the nationalism of his time not as worthy to fill out a person's life but actually as annihilating his life by making man a state slave.

Socialism, too, contributes to nihilism, according to Nietzsche, since its aim is on the lowest, the purely hedonistic level. He was unimpressed by the fact that Marxism had succeeded so well as far as the number of its followers were concerned. As he had no respect for what he considered the masses, he found it only natural that the Marxist philosophy of material comfort should have such a large following. But even the most perfect Golden Age of material happiness would not mean that the specter of nihilism—the life without real meaning after the death of all creativeness—had been dispersed. In such a life, decadence, in a desperate attempt to cover up nihilism with a nice scheme, would reach a high point. Socialism would prove in the end to fail as an answer to man's total problems, because "socialism is no more than the younger brother of the nearly dead old-fashioned despotism, which he wants to succeed. In its very core it is reactionary, since socialism strives for such a scope of governmental power as only despotism has held before. It even goes beyond despotism by striving after the annihilation of the individual, this individual which for socialism is an unjustified luxury of nature and which it wants to transform into a functional organ of the human community."[12] But tragically and paradoxically socialism claims—and probably believes itself—to strive to use society as a means to the utmost happiness of the individual.

Christianity—pinnacle of decadence. After these criticisms of scientism and the ideologies of the nineteenth century, which, not in their content but in their tenor, parallel much that existentialists said later on, one might suspect that Nietzsche would call for a retreat to earlier European thought. To do this would have amounted to an endorsement of Christianity in one way or other. But on the contrary, Nietzsche directed his sharpest criticism against this very Christianity, or to put it more accurately, against the Christianity he had experienced. This had been the pietistic version of Lutheranism practiced by the ladies of the Nietzsche household who had sheltered his youth. It included also the official Lutheranism of Northern Germany and to a lesser extent the Roman Catholicism of Central Europe. This is stated not in order to depreciate his criticism but as a reminder of the inexactness of the term Christianity.

Some of Nietzsche's criticism, as a matter of fact, was not at all new. The accusations that the close alliance with the State had corrupted Christianity and sanctioned many an unchristian venture had been uttered many times before. Quite Kierkegaardian sounds the lament that of Jesus' attempt to found the kingdom of God in the hearts of men had developed churches as instruments of salvation and originators of doctrines. On the other hand Nietzsche asked the liberal Protestant whether it was really possible to have a Christian ethics and discard Christian metaphysics at the same time. But all of this is not the central concern of Nietzsche. His real objection to Christianity is much more fundamental. It is essentially a question of his interpretation of mores and morality. According to him, "Customs (mores) represent the collective experiences of bygone generations with regard to what is useful and harmful—but morality does not refer to these experiences as such but rather to the age, holiness, and unquestioned acceptance of the customs. And these feelings prevent man from making genuinely new experiences and from changing his customs. This means that morality obstructs the creation of newer and better customs—it makes man dull."[13] It is the charge that Christianity had developed into a tranquilizer for man which Nietzsche hurled against it. He accused Christianity of remaining on the plane of mere morality, as in codes of conduct which require adherence, rather than stimulating creativeness out of one's full personal life. Thus Christianity sins against the very principle of life itself which demands that creativeness go on as long as there is life in this world. To throttle this creativeness in man by forcing him merely to accept the products of bygone acts of creativity is to kill life itself. Decline sets in as the vengeance of violated life. This does not mean that Christian morality had not contributed important and positive elements to European culture: the value of the individual, the meaning of evil, and the stressing of the dignity of human life. But over the centuries Christian morality had killed the personal and creative element in morals. It had kept on soothing man so efficiently with its creeds and formulas that he had not seen nihilism, this "uncanniest of all guests," at the door or even in his own heart. Christianity serving such a function is, in Nietzsche's terminology, an instrument of decadence. He was convinced that Jesus himself would deny such a following. Jesus was the only real Christian. His real message was his life in which he wanted to set an example of how noble human life can be. His was the message of the practice of love. What was called Christian in the nineteenth century, its preoccupation with a formalism of salvation and official creeds, Jesus would have denied. Nietzsche sounds like an even more radical Kierkegaard when he characterizes heaven as "an inner occurrence rather than being above the earth or an event on the calendar of history."[14] What happened after the end of Jesus' life, especially the writings of the New Testament, Nietzsche called a fraud. The New Testament is nothing but a seduction to see in Jesus the ideal of meekness in order to create a soothing Christianity and a submissive Christian. Both attempts were objectionable to Nietzsche who felt himself to be the prophet of a new era. A soothing Christianity offers a body of sacred knowledge which is used as ointment for the burning unrest in man. Man accepts it and becomes satisfied, but at the same time dies as a creator. While this criticism superficially resembles that of Kierkegaard, the criticism of the fostering of submissiveness is radically different. To accept God and submit to his will was for Nietzsche (as later it was to be for Sartre) the same as to abandon man's freedom. God implies divine providence and divine providence leaves no room for human freedom. Only in a world where there is necessity but not harmony can man be a creator. Only in a world of chaos in the sense of aimlessness can there be true creation.

The Christian existence, which for Kierkegaard was the highest possible form of human life, Nietzsche would have found partially a step in the right direction since it freed man from a life of mere conforming to codes and dogmas. But Kierkegaard led man to the precipice to let him discover God in a personal confrontation. Nietzsche wanted man to go to the precipice in order to discover the world in the abyss below as a chaos. Then a few at least would become really free and fulfill Nietzche's dream of the "Higher Man" (often called Superman or Overman). Consequently every attempt to prevent man from glancing into this boiling chaotic abyss, whether Christian or otherwise well-intentioned, constitutes decadence per se.

Truth lived versus objective truth. The quest to go "beyond" has, on the Nietzschean path, led man to confront nihilism as the last consequence of the European intellectual development. Given the courage to break through the various layers of decadence which desperately tried to hide this phenomenon, the European of that period arrived at the same time at the horrifying and challenging insight that the world is intrinsically a chaos lacking any pre-established meaning. "The general character of the world, on the other hand, is to all eternity chaos; not by the absence of necessity, but in the sense of the absence of order, structure, form, beauty, wisdom, and whatever else aesthetic humanities are called."[15] Meaning can only be brought into this world by man. But how is man to do this? Where is the answer which in itself is not decadent, that is, which is not again an escape from this insight, one which is truth but not necessarily a consolation?

Nietzsche, like Kierkegaard, states that systems of thought seen as carriers of objective truth cannot be the solution. They cannot endow man's life with meaning, nor are they the verbal incarnation of truth. Between the symbols of a system and the fullness of reality itself lies an unbridgeable gulf. Much of the fullness of life evaporates in the process of verbalizing it. Systems can thus be valuable only as plans or tools for living. Or as Nietzsche put it: "Truth is that kind of error without which a certain species could not live. Its value for life is the ultimate authority for truth."[16] But if man takes systems to be more than pragmatic tools he is in danger. Nietzsche, who liked to express himself bluntly, called the building of systems for other than purely pragmatic purposes dishonesty. This is because man is all too apt to forget that each system rests on accepted but not proven propositions. Intrigued by the wonderful coherence of his system—which is after all only coherence and not truth—man ends up with a world view turned into a conviction, which he holds fast for the rest of his life. Yet, contrary to general opinion, intellectual courage is shown not in the faithful and perpetual affirmation of certain convictions, but in the willingness to continuously test these convictions. Thus against the acceptance of systems Nietzsche puts the tireless questioning of the core of life itself as the truly human task. Accordingly, again foreshadowing existentialist views, he declares truth to be an endless process. It is creative in itself since it does not consist in passively becoming conscious of something which occurs outside oneself. Truth in Nietzsche's terms is creative commitment, actively determining the world. Objective truth, requiring dispassionate search and longingly sought after for centuries, is unattainable in this world. Truth is personal and highly subjective. It opens up only to questions put in the most personal manner, such as "what exactly is it that I do?" Nietzsche therefore considered that the Western experiment—beginning with the early Greek philosophers, especially Socrates—to exclude every aspect of man except reason from the truth-finding process was a fatal mistake. Thought without passion is another road to decadence. The result of such an endeavor is the very systems which kill human spontaneity and creativity.

Nietzsche's analysis of truth came even closer to the existentialist viewpoint when he scornfully described both the thinkers who build systems without intending ever to live according to them, and those people who accept knowledge about something without its having any consequences on their lives. Such people even view a man who takes his intellectual responsibilities seriously as abnormal. But in truth it is only such a man who will fulfill man's most worthy task "to become who he is" (*Du sollst werden der Du bist*). He will constantly surpass himself, remaking himself ever anew. Although he will never find rest and security, he will be free from despair. With truth recognized as an endless process, the world, as Nietzsche saw it, becomes again infinite and ready to be formed by man. The philosopher far from being a builder of systems of thought becomes a creator and prophet. Philosophy, as the search for truth, is no less than the will to create the world. To be a philosopher is "to learn to dance on the verge of abysses." Into these abysses the old disappears and out of them comes the new. Radically honest as he was, Nietzsche did not exclude his own philosophy from this process.

As has already been indicated, the strongest argument that truth is a process lies in the fact that the world itself is such a continuing process. In relation to such a world man is not merely a something always present, sometimes inactive, sometimes active. On the contrary, in Nietzsche's words, he *is* action. When Descartes gave modern Western philosophy the leitmotiv "*cogito ergo sum*" (I think, therefore I am), he introduced a tragic error. The action of thinking, according to Nietzsche, does not imply that there is back of it a substance which performs the act of thinking. To infer the presence of a substance from the presence of an action is not valid. Action proves only the occurrence of action, and there the matter should rest. Thus Nietzsche would agree with some of the later existentialists who propose that man is what he does. Such a view contradicts concepts of long standing in philosophical debate. It holds, for example, that man is not fundamentally mind (the idealist position), mind is merely an aspect of man, developing with him and well integrated for that purpose. It opposes likewise the exaggerated view of matter (the materialist position). Man should be seen as an aggregate of forces uniquely shaped in interdependence with a unique environment. Somehow Nietzsche here anticipates the physics of the twentieth century with its key concept "energy" and its subordination of the concept of substance.

One more consequence of Nietzsche's view of man and the world is methodological. Nietzsche was an empiricist, though his empiricism was of necessity quite different from that characterized by observation, measurement, and the controlled experiment. Such a method presupposes not only that one knows the whole of the world in order to know the one and only method, but also that in the course of the experiment man can divest himself of all involvement in this world. The expectation of getting "data" or facts from such a procedure is an illusion, since there are no facts without prior interpretation. Against this method Nietzsche puts the empiricism which knows only experimenting with oneself and one's life.

In the process of life itself a position taken at one time will be tested and will then help build a new position. Thus life is observed by living in it fully and critically.

This marks the end of what is called the "analytical," the "no-saying" Nietzsche. He was to have enormous impact on the existentialist philosophers, as will become amply clear. Nietzsche's final answers to the problems of man are, on the other hand, comparatively less important for our purpose. They will be briefly mentioned in order to round out this discussion of Nietzsche and to shed further light on his analysis, especially since it may be instructive to compare his answers with those given by the existentialists.

Authentic existence as Promethean existence. Nietzsche hoped that his answers would not give rise to new illusions about man's position in this world and thus lead man further into decadence. He put them in three phrases, the last an ideal: the will to power, the eternal recurrence, and "Higher Man" (Overman, Superman).

The first, the will to power, has led to serious misinterpretations, partly the fault of the brilliant stylist, Nietzsche, who in this case, was surprisingly unimaginative in naming a phenomenon. He had learned from Schopenhauer about the importance of will. But he had rejected the explanation of man's life and actions in terms of a will to live. For Nietzsche it was unthinkable that life itself should be the end and aim of life. If will pervaded the world as an all-powerful force, it must be a force which aimed beyond what already is. There seems to have been in Nietzsche a hidden hope that the infinite world of his conception would give birth to ever higher forms of life. To accomplish this in the realm of man was the task not of God or any supernatural or natural process but of man himself. More concretely, it meant a challenge for each man to affirm his will to power. This was definitely not understood by Nietzsche as the will to success, wealth, or military, racial, or political power (although at certain times Nietzsche proved not to be free from such ideas). To define it exactly has been the difficult aim of many a biographer of Nietzsche. Nietzsche himself offers little help. The phrase "will to power" appears here and there in his works. In *Thus Spoke Zarathustra* he emphasized it in one crucial section ("self-overcoming"). But the book called *The Will to Power* was not even written by Nietzsche. It is only an arbitrary compilation by his sister of some of his notes. It may be suggested here that power in Nietzsche's interpretation is essentially the power to create. In order to create, man must go through a painful process, a fact which brought Nietzsche to demand extraordinary hardiness. Man must overcome himself in order to become what he is. This coordination of all of one's psychological forces rather than just one particular force toward one aim is what Nietzsche refers to as "will." Will implies, then, both a force and an aim and is not merely an aimlessly rushing stream. To put it in other words, man should strive for the truly human in himself. To do this would make him free and independent of what hampers his spontaneity and creativity, whether it be traits of character, powerful traditions, or other restraints. The will to power understood in the most common meaning of the phrase would indicate that the person exhibiting it was seeking fulfillment in his life on too low a level. Only those not strong enough truly to create would choose it.

Almost without noticing it we have begun discussing the second concept, Nietzsche's ideal, the "Higher Man." Nietzsche often seems to imply that his "Higher Man" is closely linked to the creative elite who span the centuries. This view is especially interesting since pseudo-racial interpretations have often been attributed to it. But Nietzsche did not at all believe in the racist concepts of his time, even though he used the term master race. He would never have understood or condoned the misuse of his work for the purpose of twentieth-century National Socialism. Nowhere did Nietzsche ever suggest that his ideal, the "Higher Man," belonged to or would emerge from any particular group or people. "Higher Man" is always to be interpreted as the product of man's self-overcoming, self-education to greatness, which is radically different from the supposed racial superiority of one particular group.

Despite the indication that Nietzsche saw some connection between the highest specimen of mankind of the past and the "Higher Man" of his conception, there remains his main emphasis: the "Higher Man" as a future development, as a new chapter in human history. Although man has supposedly risen from the animal level to his present status, the distance between the animal world and man is small compared to that separating man from "Higher Man." Since no supernatural event but the success of self-overcoming through the creation of a strong will to power in a few will bring about the "Higher Man," he will be just as totally integrated into the realm of nature as man has been before. Nothing supernatural will happen, but with "Higher Man" and his strongly developed will to power, a new unprecedented height will be reached in human existence. The mass man will be overcome. Though the latter has been pledging allegiance to all kinds of aims, he has really followed only one—comfortable security. In him the passion for creation has burned itself out or has never been lighted. What is left is the willingness to accept whatever public opinion preaches. The most frightful aspect of this is that the mass man would even sacrifice freedom and the right to creativity for the feeling of security. That is why Nietzsche saw in his "Higher Man" the last hope. If the mass man were ever to glimpse even a tiny part of the nihilism he was actually confronting—and eventually he would—then, Nietzsche prophesied, he would sell himself to the Leviathan of the totalitarian state in order to escape the frightful prospect and obligation of creativity. The mass man is constitutionally unable to accept the Nietzschean solution of viewing the specimens of "Higher Man" in his midst as sufficient meaning for his own life. Instead he tries to prevent their very appearance. The mass man is and has been an opponent of all that is new and harbors only feelings of resentment toward it. He is preoccupied with opposition and does it through what Nietzsche called a slave morality. This is designed to prevent anyone's rising above the level of the mass man himself. Nietzsche nevertheless hoped for the victorious emergence of "Higher Man" in the coming decades despite this determined opposition. He would bring the morality of positive creation.

Assuming that this would actually happen, and that nihilism for the time being would be defeated, what would be the aim of such a world? Would "Higher Man" usher in a Golden Age of some sort? Definitely not. To foster such hopes would be a return to old escapist theories. The world has no aim. It is "a monster of energy" with neither a beginning nor an end. The energy groups and regroups itself without loss or increase in its total amount. There is no predestined harmony. But "Higher Man" can harness this wasteful process. In his life, "Higher Man" gives meaning to this world. His creations introduce highly developed forms into the crude processes of nature. Thus, history's aim lies not in a happy end but in the highest specimens of man. But even the triumph of "Higher Man" will always be only temporary and must be renewed by others following him. What "Higher Man" creates builds no new meaning or satisfaction into human history once and for all. The creations themselves eventually run into nothingness; only the act of creation itself gives meaning. The world process in its totality is meaningless. It consists of the eternal recurrence of regroupings of energy. And thus only the existence and the work of "Higher Man" makes for a truly human history. Without it only despair is left. Can it be denied that Nietzsche drove atheism to its honest and farthest conclusion?

Nietzsche's "Higher Man" and his will to power have not found their way into existentialism. But the way Nietzsche struggled to find these concepts and even some of their features have left marked impressions on the work of all existentialists. There is Nietzsche's keen awareness of modern man losing himself in the routine of a highly developed civilization, and awareness also of the many forces which encourage this dangerous loss of true personality. The "isms" with their promises of everlasting progress, of happiness as a citizen of a national state, of the coming of the ideal society; the so-called scientific world views with their degradation of man into an insignificant part of animate or inanimate nature; or official Christianity with its view of man as a carrier of creeds and dogmas, are all unmasked as anti-individualistic. None of them encourages man to look into himself and search for what it means to be plainly and truly himself. Tragically all too many liked these deceptions, since the alternative, the *werde der Du bist* (become the one you are), promised no shelter, no feeling of security, and no easy explanations. The truth obtainable for this "single one" demands activity, creativity, and personal involvement in what one does. In short Nietzsche, apart from all of his specific ideas, challenged his contemporaries to see and admit that, despite national glory and material progress, it is still the individual existence which is at the core of all that is human: to fail there is to fail as a human being. When Nietzsche finally despaired of ever being able to bring at least a few of his contemporaries to this insight, he had forgotten what he himself had once written: "At the bottom, every human being knows very well that he is in this world just once, as something unique, and that no accident, however strange, will throw together a second time into a unity such a curious and diffuse plurality: he knows it but hides it like a bad conscience—why? from fear of his neighbor who insists on convention and veils himself with it. But what is it that compels the individual human being to fear his neighbor, to think and act herd-fashion, and not to be glad of himself? A sense of shame, perhaps, in a few rare cases. In the vast majority it is the desire for comfort, inertia—in short, that inclination to laziness of which the traveler spoke."[17]

C. Critics of the "New Era" in the Sciences, Arts, and Literature

Kierkegaard and Nietzsche nearly overpower the other critical voices of the nineteenth and twentieth centuries. There were, nevertheless, many of them from the fields of the sciences, arts, and literature alike. They, too, contributed to the gradual destruction of the overconfidence of modern man concerning the validity of what he knows and does.

1. SIGMUND FREUD

One significant sign of the upheaval in man, or at least of the fact that the depths of human existence had not been exhausted by the contemporary sciences, was the development of psychoanalysis by Sigmund Freud. Man, as Freud viewed him, is a stranger to the idea of a wholly civilized world. He is born into this world with wild, untamed passions bearing the all-pervading libido (a life-force prominently expressed in the sex desire). This untamed man, the "id," as Freud called him, is then slowly and forcefully molded by his society and its agents (corresponding to the "super ego" of man's personality) into a smoothly functioning social being (the well adjusted "ego"). But this smoothness is mostly superficial. In reality man is still full of complicated processes. The wild passions of the "id," denied an outlet in the conscious sphere, continue to assert themselves in intercourse between the conscious and the unconscious. Even the mere stipulation of a sphere of "unconsciousness" adds a new dimension to man, one of infinite complexity. This sphere, the processes supposedly going on in man, the complexes, and the assumption of a surging and irrational elementary life force can hardly be reconciled with the idea of a definitely and unalterably civilized man. Still Freud had breathed too deeply of the optimism of the nineteenth century to be able to admit that the problem of life is bottomless. He was convinced that through proper psychiatric engineering a smoothly functioning man and society could still be achieved. As a matter of fact, Freud already knew, as Freudians since have known, that man's liberation from his fundamental problems is really never farther away than the nearest psychoanalyst.

2. MODERN ART

Another storm signal, this one closer to the existentialist spirit, became visible in what is still called modern art. Great art had always sought to catch life at its fullest and deepest, but not since the Renaissance had there been such a surge of experimentation and deliberate defying of the old and the traditional. This was not just innovation for its own sake. The modern artists were trying to penetrate to depths of which the art of the early and middle nineteenth century was unaware. True, each school of modern art seems to concern itself with only one aspect of life. The impressionist discovered anew the world of light and color. Cézanne strove to make the order of things in nature visible in his paintings. Naive simplicity was the professed ideal of Gauguin. There was the wild experimentation of the Fauvists, like Matisse, and the prayerful art of Rouault. Along with these went the strange geometry of life of the cubists. The surrealists produced dreamy creations of phantasy. Finally, there could be heard very early the outcries of passion and compassion of the expressionists, whether Van Gogh, Munch, Kokoschka or many others. Above them all stands the towering personality of Pablo Picasso and his monumental work. Insufficient in their aims and conceptions as these attempts were to interpret life as a whole, they nevertheless add up to an impressive act of prophesy and venture into the unknown. Modern art may have dropped some of the enthusiasm of the Renaissance and other periods for the picturing of the human body, but it has penetrated deeply into the psyche of man, and significantly its search seems endless, as befits all genuinely human endeavors.

3. WHAT OF LITERATURE?

All great literature has existentialist aspects. The question is whether in the period under discussion can be found examples of outstanding works with a strong existentialist emphasis. One must go to Eastern Europe to find the first example, in the work of *Fëdor Dostoevski.* The Western, especially the representative French, novel of the late nineteenth and early twentieth centuries was dominated by psychological and sociological realism. The writer either was intoxicated by man's internal world, particularly sex, or he was launching a crusade for a better society. With rare exceptions he did not question the meaning of life in relation to God. In line with the predominant trend of his age, he viewed man as an organism which through a complex intertwining of environmental and hereditary factors became a fascinating object to write about. His realism all too often was the realism of the slum, the sick, the poor, and the sensual. This Nietzsche once called disparagingly the "realism of the sewer." It was not so with Dostoevski. For him man is a stage in a titanic struggle of forces with cosmic dimensions. All that actually matters is this struggle which in each man has the crucial result of either losing or winning himself. And the struggle is always fought with reference to God. The reading of any one of Dostoevski's novels will dispel the suspicion that what is offered is pietistic literature or theological textbooks. Dostoevski's characters are no mere puppets to convey abstract ideas; they wrestle with those "cursed and everlasting questions" which are their problems. Out of this struggle of creatures of flesh and blood emerge Dostoevski's conceptions of man, of God, and of their relationship with each other.

For Dostoevski the core of man's being is freedom. But what a freedom it is. It has little if anything to do with the Western liberal conception of it. Freedom he considers not one of the innate rights of man, but the very condition of man's life. Far from making the human being happy, it gives his life the turbulence of a whirlpool. So burdensome does it seem to many that they happily exchange freedom, "this fearful burden of free choice," for comfort and security. To exist as a being endowed with freedom but fighting all too often in order to reject it, man becomes paradoxical, even absurd. He does not, as is popularly believed, strive primarily to gain happiness. The direction of man's life, if there is any, is dictated by his seemingly quenchless thirst to explore and to live his life to its fullest. He becomes the despair of those who want to comprehend him by the means of mathematics or physics. "You see, gentlemen, reason is an excellent thing, there is no disputing that, but reason is nothing but reason and satisfies only the rational side of man's nature, while will is a manifestation of the whole life, that is, of the whole human life including reason and all the impulses. And although our life, in this manifestation of it, is often worthless, yet it is life and not simply extracting square roots."[18] It is worse when scientists try not only to understand man in their own terms, but want to fit him into their preconceived opinions. Then they use restraint and coercion to gain conformity. The man of the Underground of one of Dostoevski's short novels protests against this with his whole life. "You believe in a palace of crystal that can never be destroyed—a palace at which one will not be able to put out one's tongue or make a long nose on the sly. And perhaps that is why I am afraid of this edifice, that it is of crystal and can never be destroyed and that one cannot put one's tongue out at it even on the sly."[19]

To deprive man of his liberty means to deprive him of his being man. Such an attempt is always directed against the dignity of man whether made by a well intentioned humanitarianism or a particular brand of Christianity. None has the right to stop an individual's search for a meaning to his life—his most profound expression of freedom—just because the restrainer thinks he has found answers he cherishes. "This craving for community of worship is the chief misery of every man individually and of all humanity from the beginning of time. For the sake of common worship they have slain each other with the sword. They have set up gods and challenged one another, 'Put away your gods and come and worship ours, or we will kill you and your gods.' "[20] So freedom must be taken as the tragic gift it is. It must be accepted with its reverse side which spells evil and destruction. Nowhere has the metaphysical dimension of Dostoevski's writing been shown so clearly as in his discussion of evil. For Emile Zola evil was an essentially sociological phenomenon, while man—or at least his hero or heroine—was intrinsically good. Dostoevski's characters are seldom so simply constructed. Most of them are curious mixtures of hate and love, constructiveness and destructiveness, filled with hidden motivations, hard to explore, and with all of these characteristics well intermingled. Man appears as a puzzle with two valid answers: sin and greatness. The term sin is used instead of evil, because in Dostoevski's thinking they are identical. And identical they are, since while freedom and evil are linked together they both need God in order to be meaningful. Without him everything becomes possible, and all values disappear. Murder becomes a natural occurrence no more important than the falling of a leaf or the destruction of a flower by a trampling foot. In this light the experience of freedom is either the beginning of faith or the end of man as man.

In this approach, the image of God also changes. It becomes more nearly like that of Kierkegaard. God does not and will never arise out of theological propositions; he emerges with living man in the totality of his life. Man in his struggles can find in God the only authority to which freedom can be tied without being abolished. God alone is great enough to give man freedom well knowing that it will be used to defy his own authority. Boldly Dostoevski even suggests that, in reverse, God exists because freedom and, thus also necessarily evil, exists. In a world without freedom however beautiful and righteous, God would be no more than another interesting piece of the inventory. God, man and freedom stand in a dynamic relationship full of momentous tensions. To abolish these tensions may look attractive but leads to the death of both God and man. To bridge the gulf between the personal God and man confronting him, however, is possible through love. And the symbol of God's love for man is Jesus Christ, who in turn is the supreme challenge for man.

Dostoevski tried to show the consequences of other proposed solutions to man's problems. They could all be subsumed under the general category of utopias of happiness. The laissez faire liberal at least never threatens to coerce; but he, too, will be disappointed. The natural harmony of the world and the idea of never-ending progress by which he sets so much store will both turn out to have been beautiful mirages. The socialist—and here Dostoevski meant various non-Marxist socialisms—worships a more dangerous illusion. Ignoring the metaphysical dimension of man and the problems deriving from it the socialist views man's predicament as primarily economic in nature. His ideal of a just society, one with a perfect distribution of goods, he relentlessly pursues. And Dostoevski feared that thousands of his fellow men would be killed in order to usher in the "new era." But, tragically, after all the destruction of life and property, instead of the ideal society would appear one in which freedom had been sold for the comforts of food and shelter.

All of these utopias of happiness will of necessity fail in the end since they are built on a faulty picture of man. Happiness only looks as if it could be easily defined. The interpretation of it as a life of comfort, upon which so many seem to agree, will be negated by the very man they have seen striving for it. All of these schemes will either have to admit failure or in defiance erect a ruthless tyranny with freedom for only a few. And what will there be for the many? The Grand Inquisitor in *The Brothers Karamazov* describes their lives: "Yes, we shall set them to work, but in their leisure hours we shall make their life like a child's game, with children's songs and innocent dance. Oh, we shall allow them even to sin; they are weak and helpless, and they will love us like children because we allow them to sin."[21]

Clearly there are in Dostoevski a good many of the existentialist themes. To mention a few of them: the disregard for the "thought out" as against the lived; life as a drama and struggle rather than a smooth organic existence; insistence on the terrible freedom of man and the responsibility resulting from it; the call for authenticity, here directed toward the finding of God; and finally the conception that the world and man's life cannot be pressed into the mold of a logical system.

It should perhaps be mentioned that Dostoevski's own concrete proposals for the shaping of human life come as a definite anticlimax. Not being needed for our purpose they deserve scant attention. Quite paradoxically, Dostoevski was an apologist alike for the Russian *ancien régime*, the Czarist state and the Orthodox Church. And in good Slavophilic manner, Mother Russia quite clearly emerges as the hope of mankind.

No other writer quite like Dostoevski appeared in West and Central Europe. But this region did not lack outstanding authors who dealt with themes close to those of existentialism. One of these was the unique *Franz Kafka.* His short life of forty-one years (1883–1924) was filled with searching and suffering. Like Kierkegaard he had been engaged and had dissolved the engagement because he saw marriage as a problem he doubted that he could and should master. Like Kierkegaard and Dostoevski he was a realist, a psychological empiricist, and an exact observer of man and his problems. But though these traits can be generally agreed upon, each reader must find his own interpretation of Kafka's works. He wrote in a fragmentary style as if to leave the beginning and end of his stories open for the stream of life to pulsate through them instead of being artificially frozen and thus distorted. Every element of a story, and the story as a whole, leaves room for numerous interpretations. This has all too often been viewed as a purely literary matter. In truth it is a philosophical one, and as such one of Kafka's main connections with existentialism. It could even be said that Kafka's work will cease to live on the day when someone finds out what each writing "exactly means." The greatness of Kafka lies in his ability to write in the form of pure challenge. That is writing which does not require of the reader any knowledge of what the author intended to say, but which in the process of analyzing it, leads him instead to understand his own life. So Kafka writes stories with content but without a clearly spelled-out message.

This essential feature of Kafka's art becomes obvious if one tries to summarize some of his novels. In *The Trial* Joseph K., the hero, is accused of a crime he has not committed and the nature of which he is never able to discover. His feverish attempts to gain clarification fail. He is vaguely warned about a sentence which has been pronounced and finally is stabbed to death. K., the hero of *The Castle*, who comes to a village as a surveyor in the employ of the castle but is never permitted to reach the castle or find out anything about its people, though they influence his life. All he gains is a temporary stay in the village before he dies. These plots read like mystery stories without proper endings. But once he gets into the novels themselves the reader soon discovers that he is looking into a mirror of human life. He feels gripped, and the separating line between him and the respective character fades. He discovers that he is reading about himself by means of the superb use of indirect communication. If one of the general aims of existentialism is the communicating of deep and important experiences without dulling for one's fellow man his own genuine contact with life, Kafka by virtue of his style alone ranks as an existentialist par excellence in the field of literature.

But there are also direct ties between Kafka and existentialism. Kafka, for example, shows man enveloped in a network of interdependence with a world into which he has been thrown and in which he walks as a stranger. Everything he does has consequences, some intended and some quite unexpected and obscure. Man's actions count, even if they have unwanted and unexpected repercussions. To act always means to venture. As a matter of fact, Kafka's characters obviously fail in what they try to do. And still one is left wondering what else they could have done and whether their failures were final. Beyond this one finds them feeling lonesome, anxious, and longing for clarity. But those who guide their earthly destinies, the bureaucrats, secular and religious, are a puzzle in themselves. Instead of helping man they are most likely to entangle him in great difficulties. Kafka quite definitely harbored a distaste for officials of all kinds because he questioned their supposed benevolence and beneficence. In the religious sphere he suspected them of hostility toward the never-ending search for God which for Kafka constituted religion. The official opposes this search since he represents the known and agreed upon. Not that man has no part in the conformity propagated by all bureaucracies. It is his longing for clear-cut and simple answers which provides the fertile soil for conformity. Too many have refused to face the terrifying labyrinth of the world upon which Ivan Ilyich had looked after his easy explanations had collapsed. But each story by Kafka brings the reader back for another glimpse into it. Never does the world fully reveal itself to him, as is shown in Kafka's preference for the fragment. After each glimpse man in his concern about his life thirsts for another, but all of them together leave him deeply puzzled. What and where is the window which offers an opportunity for such occasional glimpses? Like Kierkegaard, Nietzsche, Dostoevski, and the later existentialist philosophers, Kafka answers that it is man himself. Accordingly his writings are entirely concerned with man and his inner struggles. But in spite of this he is not a mere writer of psychological or sociological novels and stories. For Kafka, in true existential manner, man and what occurs in him and happens to him is the only available door to the world.

Another example of existentialist thinking in literature is afforded by the creator of some of the West's most profound poetry, *Rainer Maria Rilke*. He is second to none in his never-tiring search for the mystery of life. In him as in Kafka, the experience of estrangement brings about an inexhaustible self-exploration, an avoiding of dogmatic short cuts, and a fight against superficial conformity. Rilke experiences and expresses profoundly the strangeness of the world which man confronts in loneliness. Strikingly similar to what Heidegger later on wrote is Rilke's treatment of death, whether it be in the *Stundenbuch* (*Book of Hours*), in his *Sonnets to Orpheus*, or in his major work of prose, the *Notebooks of Malte Laurids Brigge*. In the *Notebooks* he complains that "the wish to have a death of one's own is growing ever rarer. A while yet, and it will be just as rare as a life of one's own. Heavens, it's all there. One arrives, one finds a life, ready made, one has only to put it on."[22]

What Rilke implies here recurs as a theme in existentialism over and over again. The *grosse* and the *kleine Tod* are differentiated as in the one case death which appears as an occurrence meaningfully integrated into a person's life and in the other a merely incidental, seemingly senseless destruction of life.

Finally, there is the great figure of the Hispanic culture,

Miguel de Unamuno. Reading his work *The Tragic Sense of Life* produces the impression of listening to an overture to existentialism. Here are the themes, the tonal color, and behind the curtain the stage is set. One needs only to look at the title of the first chapter, "The Man of Flesh and Bone," to sense the kinship. And what a man of flesh and bone he is, pervaded by a hunger for immortality, craving for it as Fyodor Pavlovitch does in his discussion with his atheistic son, Ivan.[23]

> "Ivan, and is there immortality of some sort, just a little, just a tiny bit?"
> "There is no immortality either."
> "None at all?"
> "None at all."
> "There is absolute nothingness then. Perhaps there is just something? Anything is better than nothing."
> "Absolute nothingness."

This all-powerful hunger introduces the tragic element into human life. It calls upon both reason and faith for its satisfaction. But instead of finding consolation man's whole being is burst asunder. Reason inevitably leads to skepticism and thus away from a promise of immortality. Faith could present the hope for immortality if it were not for the everlasting, torturing questioning of its validity. And so man becomes the battlefield over the great question of "wherefore does everything exist? Wherefore? It is the wherefore of the Sphinx; it is the begetter of the anguish which gives us the love of hope."[24] It is always the I which is involved, always a personal experience. For those who are repelled by the seemingly egocentric approach, Unamuno asks what this I is, and then quotes Oberman: "For the universe, nothing; for myself, everything." The hunger for immortality is a burden each man must carry for himself. Faced with "this terrible mystery of mortality, face to face with the Sphinx, man adopts different attitudes and seeks in various ways to console himself for having been born."[25]

Some just stay indifferent, try to idle their lives away until they at last plunge into deep despair when facing the "Sphinx." Others scurry to the deceptively secure-looking shelter of dogmas and doctrines. But dogmas fill man with dead images, and dull his keenness for inquiry, make him obedient and willing to accept what is offered to him. And what about the philosopher who had a glimpse of the mystery of mortality? He too often resembles Descartes, for whom doubt was "purely theoretical and provisional—that is to say, the doubt of a man who acts as if he doubted without really doubting."[26] Like Kierkegaard, Unamuno calls for the existential thinker, one who "thinks" with his whole personality and with commitment. Any other philosopher, however great he may be, is a mere caricature of a man. Philosophy is not a playful contemplation of the world but the science of the tragedy of life, a reflection upon its tragic sense. Are there any positive suggestions aside from this analysis? Unlike Dostoevski, who in his answer fell back on traditional institutions for consolation, Unamuno remained the staunch, searching, and indomitable individualist he called for. The task of the individual is to build for himself a unique life away from the mainstream of conformity. What is the reply to the hunger for immortality? There is only the Promethean demand that a life of high ideals and goodness should not end in total annihilation. For nothingness actually to be man's fate after death would be unjust; it might also be called a final, tragic triumph of man over the order of his universe, whatever it then may be.

This is a panorama of the protest which virtually coincides with the slow development of existentialism. Clearly this protest was not directed against just a single feature of the society or thought of the nineteenth and early twentieth centuries. Nor was it intended to bring about improvements in this or that aspect of European society and culture. The thinkers all protest against the very assumptions on which the heralded "new era" of European history was supposed to rest. They protest against optimism concerning the cultural refinement of man and faith in the progress of mankind, against the expectation that the "Golden Age" of knowledge, comfort, and wealth would result from the rapidly developing sciences and technology, and finally against the tendency to see in the modern mass society a home unsurpassed in giving man a feeling of security. Most of them, Kierkegaard and Nietzsche in particular, refuse to discard these hopes lightly as the incurably naive optimism of a species which continues to hope even after all of its hopes have been constantly shattered.

Kierkegaard, Nietzsche, Dostoevski, and Unamuno all reveal a strong sense of involvement in this world. From this feeling arises their deep concern that all of the assumptions cherished by modern man have led and will lead him to forget the most fundamental of all questions, the meaning of human life. They are not concerned with man as a functioning member of society and are not interested in supposedly final answers supplied by science, dogmas, and ideologies. Their question is put to the unique I which stands in a historically concrete but deeply mysterious world. Whether their answer finds the authentic human life in the Christian existence (Kierkegaard), in the assertion of man's will to power (Nietzsche), or in a life of heroic pessimism (Unamuno), they all center the attention upon that depth of the human life which their contemporaries preferred to neglect. It is only fair to point out that none of them acted out of personal resentment against his society. As a matter of fact, Kierkegaard, Nietzsche, and Unamuno could have led pleasant and sheltered lives as well-cared-for citizens of their respective countries. Their protest came from a much more profound level than that of resentment, namely that of genuine concern for what it means to be truly human. Not being mere *ad hoc* critics of some specific deficiencies of their societies they were thus able to become the source of inspiration for much of the thought of the twentieth century.

III. Existentialism Arrived

A. The Challenge—
The Age of Disenchantment

At the turn of the century few Europeans doubted that they were traveling on the high road to the Age of Happiness and Plenty. There were reasons enough to think so. The cities had grown into centers of flourishing economic and cultural life. Man's working conditions had become progressively more humane. Educational and health services had achieved a level never before known to man, and from the thousands of industrial plants issued a constant flow of new, comfort-producing products. Perhaps even more encouraging was the seeming certainty of having climbed to heights of civilization from which there would be no going back. Although the Europe of the year 1900 did not offer a picture of complete harmony, chaos seemed finally to have been relegated to the past. But then came the year 1914. It seemed to begin rather harmlessly with one of those wars into which one marched with a band to fight battles, gain both glory and some territory, and finally return home to lead a "normal" life. But the route of this march led straight into the greatest holocaust of history, and now after nearly half a century has passed no one yet knows whether the end of it has come. During it man underwent physical and mental terror to an extent hitherto unknown. One horrible, unbroken line led from the trenches of the First World War to the barbarism of the modern concentration camp with its deliberate extinction of millions of human beings. Instead of the expected better world man found one where he was confronted by the combined threats of atomic devastation and the totalitarian state. In place of a just world order there came "the brotherhoods with the aim of robbery and exploitation of the non-brothers" which Nietzsche had predicted decades before. But it had been the custom to ignore Nietzsche as a dreamer, disregard his work as the delusions of an insane mind, or tailor what he had said to one's needs. After all, what respectable thinker would leave his work to the world without ordering it into a system? Still, the popular practice has been to claim that all of this happened through no fault of the common man and without proper warning. The first claim is obviously wrong. The illusions cherished by man concerning the possibility of simple solutions for the human problems had a good deal to do with all the happenings. On that, more will be said. Nor could man claim that he had no warning. The works of Kierkegaard and Nietzsche both contradict such an assertion.

Soon after World War I the prevalent mood in Europe changed. Now the exalted hopes gave way to deep and dark despair. The outstanding symbol of this change was Oswald Spengler's *The Decline of the West* (1919). Elaborately written and given a name which appealed to the mood of the period, it became something of a basic book for the age. Instead of seeing a straight, unbroken line of development to heights of progress, Europeans began to speak of the birth, blooming, and decay of cultures. The words decay and decline now came readily to the lips of people who before had talked about the heights of mankind. Seldom has history seen such a sudden turn. This turn brought about an interest, although not always the most profound, never before shown for those thinkers who had until then been neglected. Kierkegaard became the great influence in Protestant theology. Nietzsche was rediscovered in a new although not altogether correct meaning. Freud's work became a serious challenge to psychology as it provided the central themes for much of literature and for pseudo-scientific discussions. Even the modern artists, much derided until now, found more appreciation of their endeavor. Too much of this new interest was obviously just a change in the popular mood, which was to shift again with ensuing historical events. Some of it, however, was a sincere look by modern man into his puzzling and terrifying predicament. In this serious search existentialism has played a leading role. And since the full blossoming of existentialism began at about that time, existentialism has often been interpreted and criticized as being just another of the products of the mood of the time. Superficially this is easy to do, since existentialist writing is full of such words as anxiety, despair, being-thrown-into-this-world, and forlornness. But little as the thinkers who prepared the way for existentialism intended to set the scene for just a change of popular mood or even a fad, modern existentialism itself has a much sounder basis.

Existentialism is not as detached from the mainstream of philosophy as some of its critics assert. Indeed it represents rather a recalling of the very purpose of philosophy itself. Philosophy has always had two divergent tendencies. One has been fervently to question the meaning of the world and of human life, unrestrained by myth or dogma. The other has been to provide the answers, so marvelously presented in the great systems of thought. These answers were man's momentary victories over the stormy restlessness in his soul. Great human achievements they were, but also fatal temptations. The danger arose when the creator of a system began to think not from the fullness of his life experience but from the basis and within the confines of the system. The temptation became even more dangerous when others, ignoring the perplexities of their own lives, chose to philosophize solely within such a system. Then philosophy exhausted itself in refurbishing the thoughts of others, correcting and criticizing thought systems. It had reached such a stage in the late 1800's and early 1900's. Lulled by an era of confidence, hard pressed by the sciences, and having retreated to the quietude of the universities, philosophy shunned its first and vital task: the radical questioning by the existing person of his own life. Existentialism restored this question to its rights and demanded that from now on it should remain in and dominate philosophy, never to be submerged again for any length of time in answer systems. This explains why existentialism had to stand in opposition to other schools of philosophy, even those which themselves were protests against the tenor of philosophy at that time: life-philosophy and phenomenology.

Life-philosophy was first to protest against the prevalent image of man during the late nineteenth century. This image showed man governed by laws which were valid alike for him and for all of nature. Consequently to study man was just to study another piece of nature. The mystery of man would disappear (at least supposedly so) in the course of scientific analysis. The inventory of nature showed no elements in man different from those present in nature. The life-philosopher put against this his concept of life as an entity. Life he interpreted as a deep, inexhaustible, and ever-flowing stream. Science and logic, although both of high practical value, are nevertheless unable to comprehend life in its fullness. Like the taker of snapshots they freeze all the activities and passions of a moment into a static picture. Experiencing the full flow of life, not abstract analysis, offers man the only way to total comprehension. Then alone intuition and real creation are possible. Logic and science can find a niche in the philosophy of the *élan vital* (the underlying life-force), but should not try to take its place in the interpretation of the world. Life-philosophy also rejects the idea of a world plan inherent in so many other philosophies. It is the free and creative spirit of man which has helped to direct the course of the stream of life throughout history. This philosophy therefore becomes a staunch defender of freedom for and of man.

While the accent on the whole and the lived seem similar to that of existentialist thought, it should not be mistaken as identical with it. Existentialism is clearly different from life-philosophy in its refusal to accept even a life-force which carries man along and yet which he can use to find a comfortable way to integrate himself into a larger whole. On the contrary existentialism wants man with his creative possibilities and his uniqueness to stand alone in a world strange to him and without comforts. Nor would the inherent relativism of the life-philosophy be acceptable. According to the latter all the various moments in the flow of life are equal in importance regardless of what values are asserted in them, while for the existentialist every man should feel himself an explorer of ultimate validity here and now. In short, life-philosophy offers no possibility for an authentic existence.

Some critics have said that the two schools of philosophy resemble each other in their irrationalism. To decide whether this judgment is valid turns out to be rather difficult inasmuch as the term irrationalism carries a number of connotations which first have to be clarified. Such a clarification will be attempted later.

Existentialism has not been in harmony with phenomenology although there have been very close connections between the two trends. Martin Heidegger was the favorite student of Edmund Husserl, the founder of phenomenology, and was deeply influenced by his teacher. Sartre's study of phenomenology contributed immensely to his own philosophy. And phenomenology and existentialism do share certain basic intentions. Husserl's creation of phenomenological philosophy directly defied that trend within nineteenth-century philosophy which tried to imitate the sciences. It also forestalled claims by the sciences, especially psychology, that they were the sole interpreters of man and his world. But after agreeing in this the two philosophies go different ways.

Phenomenology never abandoned the hope of obtaining absolute certainty in its search for a system of propositions which cannot be doubted. The phenomenologist has a fervent desire to find the certain and absolutely unquestionable beginning of all knowledge, an aim far removed from the existentialist purpose which is to let each person come to the realization of his own unique existence.

The phenomenologist promptly proceeds, thus, to find and exactly describe the phenomena of consciousness. At the root of this search is a new longing for essences, i.e. for a glimpse of the underlying structure of the world. The existentialists differ. They are not interested in phenomena of consciousness alone, since consciousness can and should not be isolated from the actual existence of the whole person, nor are they willing again to reduce the individual and the unique to mere illustrations of eternally unchanging essences.

Thus, the direct lineage of existentialism still leads to Kierkegaard and Nietzsche, while there are indirect connections with other schools. In the end existentialism clearly stands out from all other contemporary philosophies. It bursts through the narrow confines of academic philosophy by its concern with actually existing man, its desire to reach each individual person and thereby to reinstate philosophy as a way of life rather than seeing it solely as an academic exercise. From this immediate concern with man derives the fascination exercised by existentialism on a Europe of turbulence, despair, collapsing traditions, and disenchantment with "isms" and dogmas, not, as often has been asserted, from such terms as despair, loneliness, nausea, and failure which existentialism uses so freely. For those Europeans who have given existentialism their assent it is not a justification for a mood of decadence but a message of restrained hope.

B. The Existentialist Triad—
Heidegger, Sartre, Jaspers

1. MARTIN HEIDEGGER: MAN—THE SERVANT OF BEING

Heidegger's key work *Sein und Zeit* (*Being and Time*) was published in the year 1927. By then Heidegger (born in 1889) had been on the faculty of the University of Marburg on the Lahn for four years. There he had come into contact with the Protestant theologians of the University, which included Bultmann and Tillich (for a short time only). Before his Marburg period he had studied philosophy under such famous German philosophers as Windelband, Rickert, and most important, Edmund Husserl. Shortly after the publication of *Sein und Zeit* he was called to Freiburg to succeed Husserl. There followed a book on Kant, and, even more noteworthy, the publication of his inaugural lecture "What is Metaphysics?" (1929). By now Heidegger had laid foundations on which much of existentialism would build, although not always according to Heidegger's plans. In 1933, Heidegger accepted the position of rector of the University of Freiburg. His inaugural address as rector shows how naive a position a great number of Germans took at that time regarding National Socialism. Or, to put it in other words, what diverse hopes were pinned to that movement. Heidegger resigned after a year of rectorship. A marked interest in the poetry of the German poet Hölderlin led to a work about him. Generally less noticed, but quite significant are the essays entitled *Plato's Theory of Truth* (1942) and *The Essence of Truth* (1943). By then Heidegger has become more, rather than less difficult to understand. This is also true of the *Holzwege* (1950; this is a German word which connotes ways through the forest which do not lead anywhere, though Heidegger doubtless did not use the word in this sense). The changes which Heidegger's philosophy had undergone since the publication of *Being and Time* are most clearly reflected in a new edition of "What is Metaphysics?" and a *Letter Concerning Humanism* issued in 1947. There "Being" itself is emphasized above everything else.

All in all, Heidegger's life is typical of a European university professor, outwardly uneventful and quietly productive. This impression is strengthened by a determined effort on Heidegger's part to withdraw and stay aloof. Today he is living such a withdrawn life in a small village in the Black Forest.

To penetrate Heidegger's philosophy proves difficult for various reasons, not the least of which is his language. Even for the native German it is full of pitfalls. It lacks the sarcastic humor of Kierkegaard and the brutal frankness of the "philosopher with a hammer," Nietzsche. Heidegger either invents new words or, more often, goes back to what he considers their original meanings. This, with his unorthodox usage of Greek and Latin terms, makes his thought all too often like a rich field surrounded by a dense impenetrable hedge.

In the following discussion every attempt has been made to render Heidegger's thought in plain English. Although this may raise some valid objections from the literalists among Heidegger's followers, it will, even with all the disadvantages which go with simplification, open the door for a good deal more understanding. Some concessions to Heidegger's language have been made, but wherever they occur they have been explained.

Existentialist or not? Another complication in the problem of understanding Heidegger's philosophy has been the argument over its classification. Heidegger, in his later years, has repeatedly rejected the designation existentialist for himself and for his work. Should he, then, be included in a discussion of modern existentialism? The answer is clearly affirmative, and the justification lies in nothing less than Heidegger's work itself. The Heidegger who denies his kinship with existentialism is the Heidegger of more recent years and, maybe, also the "Heidegger of intentions." And it is the explanation of what is meant by this "Heidegger of intentions" which is leading this discussion directly to the central question: what is the ultimate aim of Heidegger's philosophy? Some critics maintain that his purpose has shifted over the years, but actually it has been the same in all phases of his work, namely the creation of a fundamental ontology (Greek: *on*, for being, and *logos*, for theory of). This means that Heidegger has all along been aiming at a theory of Being (or reality). Why then the link with existentialism? Because Heidegger chose a new approach to achieve his aim, an approach which could be put in the form of a motto: through analysis of man to ontology. As long as Heidegger was primarily concerned with the analysis of man, he definitely bore all the characteristics of an existentialist. Only when his emphasis shifted to the second part of the motto, to the *on*, the Being, did the existentialist elements in his philosophy become somewhat de-emphasized.

The discovery of Being. Before one attempts to retrace the route of Heidegger's searching exploration through the phenomenon of man, a few initial remarks on his conception of Being are in place.

Heidegger desires, as he puts it, to go beyond traditional metaphysics. According to him this kind of metaphysics has concerned itself only with the totality of beings and not with Being as being as such. (Note here Heidegger's distinction between being and Being.) It is exactly this differentiation between Being and particular beings which is basic for his philosophy. Traditional metaphysics deals with objects, with manifestations of Being. Until now it has tried to find the last abstraction underlying all objects in the world. But this procedure is doubly wrong. First, it leaves behind the concrete world, the fullness of life, in order to discover some abstract, supposedly fundamental being as such, whether it be an ultimate substance or process. Secondly, it confuses the term being, which signifies the particular phenomenon in actual time and space, with Being as the ground of all beings. Or, not much better, it equates Being with the sum total of all beings. The metaphysicians have forgotten that prior to establishing systems of beings, with a hierarchy stretching from the supposedly highest and most important to the least important beings, what it really means to "be" must first be clarified. Whether I say "I am" or the "tree is," I indicate that I and all objects somehow participate in whatever it means to "be." Heidegger's Being refers to this mystery of the to "be." If this Being goes beyond all particular objects can it then be defined? Most certainly not, since a good deal of it and Being as a whole is concealed and can never be described. Being, as we shall presently see, can be evoked by man but cannot be put into a definition. In the image which Heidegger uses, one can say that "the truth of Being may thus be called the ground in which metaphysics, as the root of the tree of philosophy, is kept and from which it is nourished."[1] The great controversies in the field of traditional metaphysics have centered on aspects of Being (the trunk, so to speak) but have not gone into the ground in which the tree grows, into Being itself. The "soil," the nature of Being, the all important question after what it means to "be" has been forgotten. The fundamental ontology of Heidegger is then supposed to offer the foundation for all of philosophy. Can man think himself into this ground which, like the fertile soil of mother earth, gives life to all phenomena? Or as Heidegger puts it, can man discover the truth of Being itself? The answer is yes, but only by following radically new paths.

The route of the search. The aim of Heidegger is not to set a new metaphysics over against the old ones, but rather to create a philosophy which will show the involvement of this ground with all that it bears. One must be careful here not to misinterpret Heidegger. What he aims at is not the achievement of a skeleton view of the world, a skeleton of essences on which could be draped, so to speak, the less essential phenomena of the world. Nor is his Being a more or less distant relative of the *atman* of Indian philosophy. The *atman* is the world soul, in relation to which the phenomena of this world are distracting illusions, a *veil of maya.* Only by penetrating through the veil in moments of insight, mainly an affirmation of the intrinsic worthlessness of everything worldly, does man achieve a fusion with truth. In Heidegger's view Being and beings are linked together without a loss to either, though it is true that man can lose himself in the realm of beings without being aware of their common ground, Being. Although Heidegger says that man then becomes homeless and errs tragically, he does not dismiss beings as illusions. What he strives for is to bring into light the ever-present interrelations between Being and the beings. Objects, far from being depreciated, are important because they "speak" of what is hidden in them. Being "speaks" in all that "is." It is well to remember a passage in *Sein und Zeit:* "To think is to let something become visible,"[2] in this case something which we are, in which we are rooted and which completely permeates us. The search for Being is, thus, not a search for platonic essences which stand eternally and unchangeably behind our supposedly transitory world. It takes very seriously the phenomena of experience and tries to discover their meaning by relating them to their common ground, Being.

But where is there an opening which enables man to gain access to an immediate experience of Being without going through a medium like verbalization? Heidegger's answer is that this opening is man himself. As the way to Being leads through experience, potential and actual, of human living, so the way to ontology in Heidegger's sense involves the exploration of the dimensions of human life. Whereas his famous teacher, Husserl, remained within the pure and clear sphere of logic, Heidegger breaks through the circle surrounding this discipline and arrives at man himself as the path to knowledge and truth. Thus was born the existentialist Heidegger.

Man as the window. The point of departure of such an exploration of man must obviously be to ask what in the special position of man enables him to be a window through which to discover Being. Superficially man looks like many other components of the world. But this is not affirmed by a closer analysis of man's situation. The phrase *closer analysis*, of course, means existential analysis, the analysis of the connection between Being and human being. The fact that man can make such an analysis is in itself a decisive characteristic of man. He alone of all beings is concerned with his connection with Being and he alone can ask what it means "to be." Heidegger emphasizes that he aims at no more than the intrinsic meaning of the word "be." He also frequently puts it in the more common question why there is anything rather than nothing. Always, however, the questioning focuses on the great puzzle of how man himself is connected with Being, since it is here that Heidegger sees the only access to an answer. Man is that place in Being where the question about Being can be put. Heidegger refers to man as that particular being which stands as the only access to what it means to be, as *Dasein*. *Dasein* is one of the German words which Heidegger has endowed with a much more complex meaning than it has in ordinary German usage. In a literal translation it means no more than "being here." To avoid this phrase, which has little connection with Heidegger's intention, it is better to use either the German *Dasein* or the English word existence, remembering the specific meaning attached to it, namely that it stands for man as he is interpreted by Heidegger. His analysis of *Dasein*, which follows, provides a further explanation of this term.

Obviously *Dasein* (or existence) has two dimensions. One is the connection with Being which it shares with other beings. A horse, too, is a being connected with Being. But *Dasein* as specifically human existence has as its second dimension the possibility of being aware of or knowing about its connection with Being, asking questions pertaining to its own being, and thus of transcending all other beings. But this second dimension is a possibility only. Man can ignore this question and just not ask it. He can float and coast along. He can exist like other beings not knowing and not caring about his connection with Being. But *Dasein* can become authentic existence. When it does, two things happen. Man, as Nietzsche would have said, becomes the one he "is," meaning that only then is he (or does he become) truly man. And, secondly, as Heidegger puts it, only in authentic existence *Dasein* experiences Being in its immediacy. This experience comes to man in the fullness of his life and not after leaving the world on paths of abstractions. To become aware of Being involves the whole person, not just "pure consciousness." *Dasein* is, therefore, first like a closed, darkened window. Only in authentic existence is it opened. And then it is done not for a disinterested look at Being, a snapshot of a fascinating object, so to speak, but in order to gain the deepest personal experience man can have.

Is it surprising then that Heidegger attributes such importance to the analysis of *Dasein* for man's insight into himself, and for his fundamental ontology?

Not categories but existentialia. What so far had been said about *Dasein* makes clear that to analyze it never aims at finding a fixed human nature, because what is essentially the same from man to man, like his physique, is of little importance for the real question. Heidegger rules out the possibility that a set of categories can exhaust all possible knowledge concerning man. Even the best and the most cleverly designed analytic classification will fail. The proper approach is to center one's attention on the modes of human existence, called the *existentialia.*

Being-in-the-world and care. The first such mode is the being-in-the-world. This again means more in Heidegger's work than the words would seem to indicate. Western philosophy, with a few exceptions, has always viewed man as being in the world. But philosophers have interpreted this statement to mean man's being conscious of a world which he logically analyzes and brings into a system, all the time, with obvious disinterest and acting much like an observer of the earth living on another planet. Man as he actually lives, even the philosopher himself, has not been involved in the business of philosophizing. Against this stands Heidegger's being-in-the-world. *Dasein* and world are joined. They do not exist apart from each other. All attempts of various schools of philosophy to depreciate one in favor of the other gives from the beginning a false idea of what it means to be man. Heidegger rejects both cosmologies which swallow man and make him into a thing among things, and pure anthropologies which have too little regard for man's world. To begin the analysis of man with his being-in-the-world means to go back behind the artificial separation of subject and object. Only the whole man understood in total interdependence with his world provides a correct point of departure for philosophical thinking. Such central concepts as have hitherto been built, like consciousness and all-powerful reason, will have to be re-evaluated in this new light. That such a re-evaluation will not strengthen their position has already been indicated.

With the total interdependence between man and his world accepted as fundamental fact, man relates himself in new ways to both things and persons. Things, for example, are then not just there, as they are for an observer, but assume the quality of tools (Heidegger's *Zeug* and *besorgen*). Other persons are recognized as being interwoven into every man's life in social phenomena. (Heidegger's *fürsorgen.*) Both of Heidegger's words mentioned are derivatives of the German word *Sorge*, meaning care. This indicates the weight Heidegger gives to care. He sees in it the very structure of *Dasein*. Care should be understood here without emotional overtones. It is the purely factual statement of a man's relating himself to and concerning himself with something or someone. And it is of utmost importance that *Dasein* can care for itself, that is to say, can direct its life and all its inquiry into the ground of its being, into Being. This third dimension of care is, thus, the midwife at the birth of genuine existence.

The crucial fact of nothingness. At this point the question may be raised whether logical and disinterested analysis could not do as well what care with its implied deep involvement of the individual in his own life can do. Heidegger denies this possibility, since logical analysis needs the separation of the thinking subject and the thought-about and judged-upon object. Heidegger advocates the *andenkende Denken*, that is, a process of thinking which knows itself enveloped in the totality of Being. Rather than approach objects as totally strange phenomena to be isolated and represented, this kind of thinking recalls in each of its acts the truth of Being. This distinction becomes of utmost importance in the exploration of human existence and its dimensions. Logical analysis will encounter an obstacle it cannot overcome, the crucial fact of nothingness. If one thinks in terms of objects, of beings as beings, nothingness indeed is beyond comprehension. Nothingness cannot "be" in the strict sense of the word. It cannot become an object and can never be relegated to the form of an image. Still Heidegger conceives of it as more than just a mere negation, like the saying "no" to a statement, nor is it only the theoretical opposite of the sum total of all beings. On the contrary nothingness, and this is central for all of Heidegger's thought, is deeply ingrained in Being itself. It is that which opens Being up, and lets it appear in *Dasein* (in human life). Heidegger, in order to characterize nothingness and its important working formulated his famous "*das Nichts nichtet,*" —a phrase widely ridiculed and defying translation. (*Nichten* as a matter of fact is a totally new German verb coined by Heidegger himself.) The phrase can be explained, however, as stating that nothingness permeates all beings, a fact which appears when it lets them eventually disintegrate as beings. But *nichten* also indicates that Being itself came into its own only by virtue of nothingness. As a dynamic force in Being it gives birth to Being. If the objects of this world did not change at all and never were devoured by weather, floods, or man, and if, furthermore, man were like the Greek gods eternally young and immortal, the question of what it actually means to "be" would not arise. But let one being be annihilated and suddenly the world becomes mysterious. What has before been the mere fact of being changes into a mystery. A "beyond," or "beneath" (in Heidegger's spatial terms), has appeared, and it was nothingness which created the question after it. Being, as the ground of all beings, left undisturbed and tensionless, would remain silent forever. This creative role of nothingness for Being, its primordial working, is brought to life in man's existence. Man's existence, as that mode in which human life blends into its own ground, that is to say into Being, is then necessarily tied to nothingness. In this exploration, which is a matter of vital concern and not one of idle curiosity, logical analysis cannot be the ultimate guide. How else then can man gain access to nothingness and its working? By virtue of what often is called the basic moods of human personality but is much better expressed as the basic dispositions of man. In short, we return to some of the *existentialia.*

From being-thrown-into-this-world, anxiety, death, to authentic existence. There is first the disposition of being-thrown-into-this-world without one's consent. One is given a burden to carry without having been consulted. Closely connected with this disposition is man's experience of the mysterious quality of the world. Nowhere does the cleavage separating Heidegger from all philosophies advocating retreat from the world become clearer than in his demand as to what man's attitude toward this disposition should be. Far from calling for a retreat from the world, the disposition of being-thrown-into-the-world he views as a challenge to make this world really man's own. Being aware of the mystery of his existence man is to begin his efforts to lead a life open to the call of Being. Instead of enthusiastically embracing this challenge, however, man tries to escape it by making his world into a place he is accustomed to and feels at home in. This is exactly what Tolstoy's Ivan Ilyich tried to do when he drifted into his life of conformity. But man's care for his own connection with Being cannot so easily be deadened, if at all. It returns in yet another disposition, even if at times he tries to close his ears, his eyes, and his heart to it. This disposition is anxiety.

Anxiety is used here not as just another word for fear. Fear refers to the feeling of being threatened by something particular, like a thunderstorm or a dark room. Such fears may be quite unnecessary from the standpoint of an outside observer. Anxiety, however, refers to a common and basic human experience. In it the total person feels suddenly the contingency in which he lives. In anxiety man confronts nothingness. Anxiety is therefore not in any way similar to a fear caused by a superstition or a misunderstood context. It has its roots in the confrontation with nothingness and offers the way to an authentic life, to a finding of one's ground in Being, in authentic existence. In this positive evaluation of the experience of nothingness Heidegger is closely akin to Nietzsche. But Nietzsche's answer to nihilism was his call for "Higher Man." Heidegger takes another way. For him, anxiety can lift man out of the limbo of the seemingly natural condition of everyday life. In it the "one," in the sense of the mass, the average, and the officially condoned, rules. One does what the many do, one says what the many say. Even the world which one on occasion had felt to be absurd and awe-inspiring becomes familiar and spells comfortable security through the medium of a busy routine.

Many modern thinkers have pointed to the age of the mass-man with critical disapproval, but they see in it a specifically modern phenomenon. For Heidegger the concepts of the everyday and the impersonal "one" are basic modes of living, whether in ancient Egypt or in the Europe of the twentieth century. This abandonment of oneself to the everyday is, therefore, an ever-present danger. Even the person aware of it will make some concessions to it, since a certain amount of conformity is necessary for civilized life. But the danger of conformity is its tendency to grow in scope until it embraces and stifles everything. That is the reason why anxiety carries positive overtones in Heidegger's philosophy. Instead of being negative and resulting from maladjustment, as phychologists would say, anxiety is that basic disposition which grips the whole person, makes him aware of his estrangement from Being, makes him feel completely threatened, and in doing so sets free liberating forces. Not that this makes anxiety a pleasant experience. It sets man apart, gives him the awareness of being alone and thrown back on himself. Compared with this experience all other experiences become of little importance. Nor is the mode of being to which anxiety opens the door, authentic existence, a comfortable resting place. It is not surprising that man again and again tries to go back to where he had come from, namely to the comfortable world of everyday. But in doing so he leaves his potentiality for authentic existence unfulfilled. He stubbornly stays in the realm of being, neglecting man's concern with the ground of his being.

Even if man could subdue his anxiety, there is a phenomenon which he cannot entirely ignore and which is closely linked to anxiety—death. This central fact of human life, its finiteness, is disregarded by the many. For them it is merely something at the end of the thread of life which winds through the years. This is the death in the sense of a sudden and rather accidental end (like Rilke's *kleiner Tod*). But authentic existence knows only a death the awareness of which is deeply engrained into each moment of man's life. It is precisely this constant taking into consideration of death as man's most personal destiny which the average man tries to escape. He lives "as if" his life were, in the near future at least, without end. For some it is even in bad taste to mention death. Others try to dull the impact of death by finding worlds beyond death. For them death constitutes not a true end but a change from one life to another. For Heidegger all these evasive positions take from death its positive dimension. Man must realize in its full immediacy that death comes not in general ("everybody must die") but to each individual. Heidegger asks whether it is not death alone which can weave man's scattered life experience into a completed whole. If it is so, then to deny death the fulfillment of this task is to leave human life a mere collection of episodes. Death alone brings the seriousness of finitude into *Dasein*. It comes to each man in its actual neutrality. To treat death as a friend or as an enemy is equally wrong. Heidegger also declines to accept stoic heroism toward death. For him death is that fact which makes nothingness visible in human life itself, stands in each year of human life, and in doing so brings it to the threshold of authentic existence. Only in the latter does Being truly enter into the experience of *Dasein*.

Authentic existence as that state in which the interlocking between Being and *Dasein* (man's being) becomes experienceable merits thus a more detailed analysis. Heidegger once describes existence as *das Offensein für das Anwesen des Seins*. Like many of Heidegger's phrases, this one is hard to translate. A correct but awkward rendering of its meaning would be that man has to show readiness at all moments for his connection with or being rooted in Being. This might be described as the experience of suddenly reaching a clearing in a forest by which until then one had been tightly surrounded and which still only for a moment slightly recedes (Being). One senses the freedom of this clearing but only in order humbly to recognize one's deep immersion in this never-ending and all-important forest (Being). Heidegger even takes this standing-out of man out of Being as the most profound meaning of the word existence (Heidegger: *Ek-sistenz*). For him authentic existence means first of all that man endures his particular connection with Being. Man accepts this enduring as a great obligation and does not try to escape it. The question may well arise as to what the substance of such an experience is, and whether it can be described more concretely. There is no common substance. Existence is a purely formal experience, which changes one's ways of experiencing one's world rather than constituting an experience in and of itself. A parallel from the emotional life of man might be used here. A man who falls in love still lives in the same world and routine as before, but his life and the ways in which he views the world are changed by the fact "that" he has fallen in love. Authentic existence, in a sense, refers back to such a "that" experience. Here it is "that" *Dasein* has regained the ground of its Being. But after such a comparison must follow an immediate caution. Authentic existence is not an emotion or anything which one can possess or achieve in any final sense. Man remains always in the state of a flux. He makes ever new decisions concerning his standing with Being. He loses himself in the everyday world, but the call of his conscience reappears in anxiety, which tells him that he owes more to himself than he is admitting at that moment. He feels guilty if he has once denied his openness for Being and, thus, has estranged himself from Being. He will again have to risk the leap as a total person into authentic existence.

An analysis of time. Heidegger had called his main work *Sein und Zeit* (*Being and Time*). And with finitude occupying such a key place, it is not surprising that Heidegger had to turn to a re-interpretation of the concept of time. The idea of time as either a line running from early historic times to the distant future or as a mere fourth dimension in physics cannot be brought into accord with Heidegger's views of man. The radical fact of finitude would lose a good deal of its impact if man would feel that he is being carried safely along on a stream of historical events which is steadily flowing toward a predetermined goal. The past, according to such a view, is either of mere antiquarian interest or is entirely forgotten, while the future is that which has not "yet" come. Individual man in the present is conceived of as living at a point separate from what has been and what will be. It is not so with Heidegger. To be man means to live in past, present, and future alike. The past is not something already detached from him, but confronts him as the situation which he has helped to form by his own decisions and acts. The future is not what does not concern him yet, but reaches deep into the present by virtue of man's finitude. Death as a certain future occurrence with an uncertain date will in authentic existence always be a part of the present moment. Time is thus radically re-interpreted. The objective time-line has given way to time as a dimension of the individual life. Past and future represent only the tension experienced in the present between the decisions already acted upon (the past) and those to be made in the face of that ever-present event, death. Only everyday man lives in a tensionless present by forgetting the past and not caring for the future. He overlooks the fact that authentic existence depends totally on temporality rightly understood, that is in Heidegger's sense.

To summarize briefly: Man is completely interdependent with his world. Yet this does not prevent his feeling of being thrown into it and being deeply puzzled by it. The structure of man is therefore care. Care directed at *Dasein* itself and its connection with Being is the very core of human life. It springs into clear awareness in anxiety and the confrontation of death, which lift man out of the everyday, the routine, and his estrangement from Being. The call of conscience is heard and may lead to authentic existence in which man finds his way back to a life of constant awareness of his connection with Being. All of this happens in the pregnant moment of the present in which past and future are full realities.

Re: existentialist or not? Besides Heidegger the existentialist there is also Heidegger the ontologist. Actually Heidegger's main work *Sein und Zeit* indicated both his ultimate aim and his points of emphasis. Originally the volume was intended to have a sequel which, with the analysis of *Dasein* completed, would deal with Being proper. But this second volume still exists only in intention. Some critics have contended that this shows the hopeless dead-end situation of Heidegger's philosophy—namely that from the analysis of existence there is no way open to the establishment of an ontology. Followers of Heidegger, on the other hand, have interpreted the absence of the second volume as an indication of the enormous problem which Being poses. They point to the writing done by Heidegger in the meantime as enough proof of the basic validity and fruitfulness of his philosophy. The smaller works referred to most definitely have a strongly ontological flavor, so much so indeed that some interpreters claim to have discovered an outright change in Heidegger's basic position.

For those who want the implications of a certain school of philosophy clearly spelled out there remains to be mentioned Heidegger's position in the field of ethics and religion.

Ethics. The ethical import of his philosophy can be shown by a paraphrase of Kant's categorical imperative: live so that at all times the awareness of and openness to Being is preserved in each act and thought. This is the same as saying that one should live authentically. Translated into action it amounts to the exhortation: do what you can and what only you can do. This should lead to a life which is "beyond good and evil," that is, one not merely guided by codes of ethics but inspired from a much deeper creative level, that of Being. Morality, thus, is not an ultimate problem for Heidegger, but one which remains quite close to the surface. Heidegger, therefore has written nothing in the field of ethics proper and cannot be expected to write about it in the future. The call for authentic existence goes much deeper. Critics have answered that although this may be so, moral codes are a good deal more specific. But for Heidegger the call to be a witness of Being remains the core of an ethics which is pure, ascetic, and in reference to Being.

Religion. The relationship of Heidegger to religion in general and to Christianity in particular has always been a fascinating subject for study. The interest this question arouses is enhanced by the knowledge that Heidegger began his career as an aspirant to the Catholic priesthood. His position toward Christianity is ambiguous. A "no" and a "yes" can be discovered in his work. The "no" does not appear, as has sometimes been suggested, in his avoidance of the term God in his writings. It occurs when Heidegger denies any transcendent or, to put it in other terms, supernatural force or agency. He is determined to stay in "this" world, and to create a philosophy of pure immanence. His analysis of *Dasein* at no point needs an opening for God. Whatever else may separate Heidegger from or tie him to Christianity, this is the fundamental rift between the two. Compared with this everything else becomes minor: that he objects to all so-called knowledge about God, since it makes God an object or a being; that he sees all talk of immortality as fantastic stories which have nothing to do with the relationship between man and God; that he dismisses all human means to get closer to God, such as ritual and contemplative exercises, as sentimentalities. All of this sounds radical, but is less diametrically opposed to Christian thought than Heidegger's insistence on immanence. God may be looked for in or beyond Being as the ground of all being. Accordingly, if

Being cannot be described as an object but only experienced by man participating in this experience as a whole person, then God also will remain a mystery out of which man lives. Into it man never can enter as a knower but in the totality of his human existence. Thus, Heidegger does not outrightly deny God but brackets him. He is convinced that in his concept of Being there is room for even the affirmation of God. Such an affirmation is a purely personal experience, although it has its roots in the ground where all the experiences of all human beings meet. So the "yes" which Heidegger says to Christian thought appears as his willingness to let such an interpretation happen. The "yes" is even fortified by the startling ease with which such a re-interpretation of Being as the Christian God can be achieved. Many of Heidegger's terms show a close affinity to those which Christian thought has been using for centuries, as, for example, anxiety, death as standing into life, the call of conscience and the guilt invoked by failure. Even so Heidegger himself, however, could hardly be expected to encourage such a re-interpretation.

2. JEAN-PAUL SARTRE: MAN—MASTER AND USELESS PASSION

In stark contrast to Heidegger's life stands that of Jean-Paul Sartre (born in 1905). Characteristically he begins his career with a novel, *Nausea* (1938), in which existentialist spirit quite clearly speaks. It is a good deal easier to understand than Heidegger's *Sein und Zeit*. Short stories and other novels follow. Then the stage becomes his platform. Always the skill of a good writer is combined with brilliant, although not on all occasions the most profound, thought. Too many people still see in Sartre a mere littérateur. They dwell on the many hours he spends in cafés, unaware that many of the great intellectuals of Europe used to find in the café both a second home and a stimulating intellectual meeting place. But the forties brought events which should dispel doubts about Sartre as a philosopher. In the year 1943 appeared *Being and Nothingness*, a work which must be counted among the most important philosophical contributions of the twentieth century whether one agrees with Sartre's ideas or not. While Sartre was spelling out in this book the main themes of existentialism, he was also, in accord with his philosophy, risking his life in the French resistance movement. After the war he published various works, among them the popular essay *Existentialism as a Humanism*. In this period also occurred Sartre's quite startling support of communistic causes, a baffling move, even if judged from his own standpoint. The events of the Hungarian Revolution in 1956 brought, however, a significant parting of ways between Sartre and official communism.

All in all one gains an impression of a life led in a sincere search for the meaning of human life, characterized by honesty and involvement.

There are reasons for discussing Sartre next after Heidegger. The link between them is closer than that between Sartre and the other of the two important German existentialists, Karl Jaspers. Sartre was and is a student of Heidegger in the Nietzschean sense, as one who does not worship his teacher but ventures out on his own. The result is a philosophy diametrically opposed to that of Heidegger not only in details but in the basic position itself. Heidegger's central concern is with Being and how man stands at the same time in and out of it. Being in its fullness and as the ground of all beings remains the great mystery. It is almost a hallowed moment when in authentic existence the connection is brought into light. For Heidegger man, as has once been remarked, is at his best a servant of Being.

Sartre's point of departure. Sartre leaves no part of this position unchallenged. He declines to accept Heidegger's Being as the basis of all beings, and rejects any view of the world as an entity which in its very core harbors some meaning apart from the one man himself creates. Being as such represents no more than the sum total of all beings. There is nothing mysterious behind it. Beings are what they appear to be. Sartre, however, accepts Heidegger's *Dasein* as the particular being of man which opens a fissure in the otherwise solid front of beings. But according to Sartre something much more radical happens in this connection than Heidegger would admit. It is not that man through this fissure can discover his root in Being. What actually happens is that out of the fissure there grows like a solitary plant in seemingly solid rock the new phenomenon, consciousness. Man is an outsider in nature because he is the seat of consciousness. It might be well to mention here that how consciousness grows out of an unreflective and silent world of beings is a problem Sartre never deals with. He apparently fears that such a discussion would lead him deep into metaphysics, a field which he has no intention of entering. He posits the emergence of consciousness out of the world of beings as an established fact or primary position. It is a fact of utmost importance, since man is no longer safely imbedded in any whole; his being stands irrevocably separated from everything which surrounds him. Whereas Heidegger's ideal was to root man again in a ground, Sartre means to strengthen and make clear man's isolation from all other beings. Man, far from being a servant of Being, will again become a master—a master of his world and of himself.

Man and his world. Most of Sartre's work is a commentary on this, his basic position, as, for example, when he attempts a new interpretation of man which is supposed to avoid the pitfalls of traditional philosophical anthropologies. Sartre rejects the old dualism of body and mind, mind and matter, physical necessity and free will, and reality and appearance as artificial separations of what in reality is a whole. It should not be forgotten that Sartre was much impressed by Husserl's concept of intentionality, according to which consciousness is always the consciousness of something. This, of course, forms a much closer link between man and his world than the earlier interpretation of a subject with a "pure" consciousness. Pure consciousness which might or might not focus on its world, gave the individual an aura of detachment. Sartre instead accepts Heidegger's being-in-the-world without accepting his Being, and insists on the inseparability of man from his world. Whereas in Heidegger's search for fusion with Being consciousness lost its central position, in Sartre it remains at the center. Sartre, of course, realizes very clearly that there must first be a man of flesh and blood before consciousness can appear. He is no idealist who imagines a mind merely enclosed in an unimportant temporary shell projecting its own world on its own screen. Man very actually lives. The objects of the world, far from being projections of a mind, are, as Sartre puts it, rather brutally true. It is from the very fact of man's being so closely linked to his world that consciousness receives even its particular structure. In each act of consciousness man is aware both of an object outside of himself and also of himself. Sartre goes even further to assert that each moment consciousness creates the meaning of both the I and the world. Meaning thus emerges only with man. The world with all its thousands of beings carries no meaning in itself. All these beings, animate or inanimate, are meaningfully integrated into no greater whole, whether a God-created world or Heidegger's oceanlike, silent Being. It might be put thus: first there was being, and being became consciousness, and then there was light.

The en-soi and the pour-soi. Man then is in the midst of a world which silently stares at him. It is this theme which Sartre develops in his famous dualism of the *en-soi* (the in-itself) and the *pour-soi* (the for-itself). The best equivalents in English would be self-contained being and conscious-being which however, at first lacks content. The *en-soi* signifies all the objects around man. They are impermeable and dense, silent and dead. From them comes no meaning, they only are.

All hopes that behind their appearance must be an essence, a *Ding an sich* (thing in itself) or any other vehicle of meaning are futile. Even living beings (except man), are mere passivity. A tulip bulb has no choice but to produce at a certain time, at a certain place, and under certain conditions a tulip. The whole world of the *en-soi* is absurd, *de trop*. It finds meaning only through man, the one and only *pour-soi*. Compared with the *en-soi* man is a strange being. He has no fixed nature, no in-itself, and his characteristics cannot be listed. To put it in a paradox: man is not what he is. He can better be compared to a shell which can and must be filled by himself at each and every moment. As Sartre expresses it: "There is at least one being whose existence comes before its essence, a being which exists before it can be defined by any conception of it. . . . What do we mean by saying that existence precedes essence? We mean that man first of all exists, encounters himself, surges up in the world—and defines himself afterwards. . . . Man is nothing else but that what he makes of himself. That is the first principle of existentialism."[3]

Man tries to escape this obligation and strives to be an *en-soi*. To be one looks so comfortable. He needs only to let things happen. He is not forced to make something out of his life since he is something already and forever, like a tree or any other object. There are the well known excuses like: I was born that way; a bad environment did it, or God had a hand in it. All of these attempts to deny responsibility and flee into the comfortable shelter of the *en-soi* are attempts to live unauthentically. To live and to pretend to be an *en-soi* is to live in estrangement from what one can be. Such attempts are rendered futile by a shattering experience which sooner or later is to be found in everybody's life, nothingness. This nothingness is not tied to Heidegger's Being in a creative relationship. Nothingness in Sartre's view spells total destruction. Nothingness is not an aid in the emergence of Being but pure annihilation. Man in his life fades into nothingness marked by death. Still it is the encounter with nothingness and the frightening certainty that it will destroy man which brings forth human freedom and with it opens the door for a life as a *pour-soi.*

To those who are attached to freedom only in a sentimental way Sartre's freedom is no pleasant experience. It is an awesome freedom in which man is immersed and it is inescapable. Man cannot choose to be free at one time and not at another. He has no choice, because he does not *have* freedom from which he can at times hide without consequences. The core of the center is that man *is* freedom. Freedom expresses the very lack of fixed content in man, his lack of being something. It points to man's obligation to make himself. To be sure man can deny all of this, but he remains free nevertheless. Every act undertaken in the state of denied freedom none the less marks a decision. Man's freedom is thus total, and the burden of it is heavy. He must carry it alone. To try to get rid of it is a delusion whether done in the direction of God, of one's fellow man or of necessary laws. Freedom is not a blessed right but a curse and a yoke. Man, Sartre says, is condemned to be free. Lest one begin to think of Sartre as a pure-bred pessimist, the creative aspect of this freedom should quickly be pointed out. In freedom man is provided with a supreme opportunity to give meaning to his own life, which before has been an empty shell. In the course of giving meaning to his life, he fills his whole world with meaning. Freedom is, therefore, the very core of and the door to an authentic existence.

The basic dispositions: nausea, anxiety, forlornness, and despair. If man wants to avoid a wholehearted acceptance of being a *pour-soi* (and more often than not he wants to) there are basic dispositions which grip him and remind him of the futility of his endeavor to escape the freedom he *is*. Sartre's nausea is one for example. Here man experiences how the *en-soi* closes in on him. The objects of the world, although dead, without will and meaning of their own, nevertheless limit man constantly. The absurdity of the *en-soi* in its totality is oppressive. A great disgust grows in man which develops into outright nausea. But in it freedom asserts itself. Very similar are the consequences of boredom. Both experiences, being far from pleasant, aid in the birth of authentic existence. Whoever looks for pleasant experiences will not find them in the asserted freedom of authenticity. Certain schools of psychology have even declared that all of these experiences are highly undesirable and to be avoided at any cost through a better adjustment of the individual to his situation.

Anxiety too is well known from the works of Kierkegaard and Heidegger. In Sartre it refers to the experience connected with acts of choice. Since these form us and commit us irrevocably, they carry grave responsibility. Anxiety is thus the twin brother of this responsibility, and is not to be separated from it. This is especially so if one realizes that one's own choices and responsibility carry beyond one's own life into the lives of others. All of this burden man inevitably shoulders alone without the assistance and co-responsibility of others.

Another disposition is forlornness. Sartre realizes quite clearly that nothing contributes more to its emergence than his denial of God. With no God who has created and is watching the world, man is left without any comforting support. Being freedom he becomes obligated to invent himself at every moment. There are no guide posts along the road of his life. Man himself builds the road to the destiny of his choosing. He is the creator. What he gets from tradition, like values and moral codes, are only the remainders of former men's decisions and acts of creativity. They hinder more than they help, since they pose as seemingly easy guides. They cannot relieve man of his destiny to create, invent, and project himself forward and to be lonesome in the process. Forlornness is thus not a deficiency which one can remedy, but a proper disposition experienced in authentic existence. "That is what abandonment [forlornness] implies, that we ourselves decide our being. And with this abandonment [forlornness] goes anxiety."[4]

Despair, another disposition, seems the strangest consequence of freedom. In Sartre despair refers to his admonition that man should act without hope. How can he do so? What Sartre actually means is that man should act without hope for any meaning and regularity in the world other than what he himself introduces. If he needs to rely upon the sun's rising for the next action, he can make assumptions in that respect. But disinterestedly to put the whole world into an ordered system of "facts" means to rely on a total order of the universe which simply is not there. Despair is at its core the knowledge and affirmation of a universe without meaning and the realization that man himself is the center of meaning and its creator. Consequently no hope exists for man outside himself. This is directed not only against those who pin their hope on God, but also against any attempt to let such things as mass movements carry the meaning of world history. The mass in this function is an illusion. Sartre here says "no" to Marxism and its reliance on the collective, the proletariat. Finally, to take despair as an excuse for a do-nothing attitude would not only be a mistaken interpretation but an outright denial of man's basic condition and obligation. Let it not be forgotten that "man is nothing else but what he proposes. He exists only insofar as he realizes himself. He is, therefore, nothing else but the sum of his actions, nothing else but what his life is."[5] *

Authentic existence in the sense of truly being man is a venture, a genuine and deadly serious one. Authentic existence is realized only in deeds which are committed alone, in absolute freedom and responsibility, and which therefore always have the character of true creation. Man is what he has done and is doing, not what he dreams, hopes, and expects. Only an understanding of this activistic interpretation of man opens the door to Sartre's concept of transcendence. The common usage of the word, referring to a world transcending ours and clearly pointing at God, had been destroyed by Sartre's basic tenets. For him man knows transcendence only in that he himself becomes the heart and center of transcendence. Man in his actions projects himself continuously beyond himself. He leaves the himself of yesterday behind the himself of today, and that of today behind the one of tomorrow. He surpasses himself constantly, and in this constant self-transcendence lies the new meaning given to transcendence. At the same time it is the climax and the last corollary of Sartre's endeavor to put man into the center as the creator. With it there is no universe left but the human. Human existence no longer carries any meaning beyond itself. To live one's existence is highest fulfillment. "Man is the useless passion," that is man is not related to or living for use by any agency, whatever its character, but he exists solely for himself and his own task.

Again, as in the case of Heidegger, we shall discuss now some of the implications of Sartre's views for ethics, social philosophy, and the problem of God.

Ethics. If man is his own measure, if he alone invents his decisions, if he is his own legislator, where then is to be found the sound foundation for civilized community living? This question has been asked in many different variations, all containing the same implied criticism. There is first the problem of seemingly unrestrained individualism. Sartre's answer is partially contained in this passage: "And when we say that man is responsible for himself, we do not mean he is responsible for his own individuality, but that he is responsible for all men."[6] In his freedom man chooses the freedom for all mankind. The freedom of others always is implied in his own. In other words by devising his own life man created the general image of mankind. This is possible since mankind is nothing fixed for all time, but is created by man at every moment and in every action. To choose to commit himself is the same as to choose to be a legislator for mankind.

Critics have insistently asked again and again whether man

is really good and benevolent enough to be entrusted with such a task. What about evil in this world? Sartre is convinced that all evil intentions originate in a denial of man's freedom rather than in the use of it. Evil thus acquires the character of lying to oneself by hiding from the call to realize the freedom that one is. Evil is bad faith or self-deception, or, even clearer, unauthentic existence. The cowards who hide behind norms, necessities, heredity, and groups (like the state, class, etc.) are responsible for evil. So are the *salauds* (a vulgar word corresponding to the English word bastards) who forcefully assert their bad faith against everybody. Sartre's fundamental and nearly exultant optimism concerning man appears when he implies and asserts that the man who acts in freedom, with concern for his own freedom and for that of others, can do no wrong. A number of critics have found this to be not only too optimistic but also not specific enough as a guide for man. They demand a more concrete statement on good and bad. This Sartre cannot give without abandoning a good deal of his philosophy, if not all of it. Against giving such specific statement stands man as the creator who, in Nietzsche's words, is "beyond good and evil." Invention and creation cannot be guided by external norms, especially when the objects of invention are these very norms. Moreover man always acts in an historical situation which is unique, a fact which gives unpredictable content to man's creation. And all that can be said is: choose in free commitment, or, what furthers freedom is good and what hampers it is bad.

The problem of the "other." Sartre's view of man as a solitary and creative individual inevitably leads him to an extremely pessimistic view of social relations. Sartre's man is too much the seat of consciousness to be a full-fledged person. Although this may seem strange coming from a famous representative of existentialism, all of the logical consequences of Sartre's view of man in the field of social philosophy lead to that assertion, beginning with Sartre's will known dictum:

"Hell, that is other people." Less dramatically Sartre has expressed it as follows: that the permanent state of man's social relations is conflict, of which the origin lies in the human incapability of fusing two subjects into a harmonious whole. In this process either man is degraded to an object in an act of possession, or subject meets subject without any degradation but loses any possibility for a fusion, since every I is essentially a closed entity for Sartre. In the first case the I is looked upon not as a subject in its freedom but as an object. In the second case every bridge between man and man is burnt. The we is an illusion, the I is the only reality. Human beings experience this failure to resolve their social problems in hatred, conflict and strife. Even love is no exception to this, although it is the most genuine longing for unity with another being. Christian existentialists and Martin Buber have pointed to this dilemma of man as the result of Sartre's overestimation of individual consciousness, which tends to isolate the individual and leaves no opening for others. They, in their turn, have tried to solve the problem by the insistence on a personal I and Thou relationship. On the other hand Sartre does not call for a retreat of man from social involvement. He himself has not led a solitary life, nor has he shied away from speaking out about French public affairs. Even his often debated co-operation with the French Communist Party, particularly until 1956, has to be viewed as growing out of what a traditional philosopher would not hesitate to call sympathy with one's fellow man, in this case the French worker. That in many ways this was a contradictory choice Sartre has finally come to realize. For this discussion not the kind but the fact of social involvement is important, because it lays bare an interesting schism in Sartre's thought. On the one side there is his genuine humanitarianism in the best French tradition, and on the other his philosophy which hedges man in so rigidly that his attempts to communicate with his fellow men are necessarily doomed to failure.

God. There remains the problem of God. Everyone knows Sartre's reputation as an atheist, and one might add, the most consistent and honest atheist in a long time. Sartre, like Nietzsche, does not demonstrate that God does not exist. With him he announces: "God is dead." Sartre, at one point, even insists that if God did exist it would make no difference from the point of view of his existentialism. Better stated, the existence of God is excluded in any meaningful sense by Sartre's view of God. Sartre himself best clarifies this statement in one of his lectures when he compares God with a supreme artisan. As a matter of fact, Sartre never sees in God, whom he denies, anything but a supernatural artisan. The concept of man is present in this God's mind, and individual man represents a mere realization of this concept. It is precisely this divinely designed purpose for man which Sartre denies. Is not man that being which first exists and in his existence designs his own meaning and purpose? If so what function could God possibly have? God has no justification for his existence in Sartre's universe and so is entirely dispensable. What nature could God have? As an *en-soi,* a being in its fullness, he would be a mere object for Sartre. But the *pour-soi* comes about only in its encounter with nothingness in freedom. A god who would face eventual destruction as man does would be a strange one. Nor can God be the freedom man is, since freedom is bound to a lack of being. Christian and Jewish thinkers have replied by accusing Sartre of seeing in God merely a world-engineer and of overlooking the possibility of a personal relationship between man and God—an encounter in love, for example, which produces commitment to God in freedom.

Whatever the position taken toward Sartre's atheism, its superiority over some of the more common varieties of atheism must be admitted. Sartre himself turns quite outspokenly against one of these, the commonplace atheist humanism. It zealously does away with God as a remainder from a period of unscientific thought in which man still needed such superstitions. In God's place it puts man, now glorified as a self-sufficient, clever organism. This man is proud of himself and gives as reasons for his pride the celebrated specimens of mankind, whether Aristotle, Leonardo da Vinci, or Napoleon. For this type of humanist such men tend to show what an illustrious race mankind is, even if he himself leads a thoroughly mediocre and complacent life. Whereas God has been declared dead, the new saints, who supposedly give an effortless meaning to each and every life, have already been born. Besides that there are supposedly self-evident values to which all mankind owes allegiance. If all of this were not enough, God still can be dispensed with, since the benevolent laws of nature and of history, like automatic progress, guarantee an ultimately harmonious world. God's disappearance is therefore hailed as man's great act of liberation. It is an atheism, as Sartre would say, at the least expense.

Sartre, however, sees quite clearly and admits that God's nonexistence is extraordinarily inconvenient for man. It takes away from him his divinely devised nature and purpose, makes him free and lonesome, and obligates him constantly to create. Man is not a well finished creature, but a desparately struggling being. That man should be the center of this world and its history is not at all determined by the organization of this world itself. The existentialist humanist will never forget that man has not yet been and will never be determined in his final form. Man is freedom, and since freedom indicates openness toward the future, man will always remain in the state of determining what he is. It is man—each man, not just the great heroes—who does this determining for himself and for mankind. While even the existentialist atheist at times may look longingly back to the times when God meant a haven of security and comfort, he knows too well the illusory character of such longings.

Note on Albert Camus. Jean-Paul Sartre's influence on intellectuals has been enormous, so strong indeed that in the minds of many he has been identified with existentialism. By now the reader undoubtedly will have discarded this error. Nevertheless Sartre has been very prominent in the intellectual world of postwar France. Around him have gathered such Sartre-type existentialists as Simone de Beauvoir and Maurice Merleau-Ponty. He also has been the great antagonist of the French Christian existentialist Gabriel Marcel. Another celebrated intellectual polarity developed between him and Albert Camus, whose position with regard to existentialism has been variously interpreted. Camus himself expressly disavowed any connection with existentialism, though there are definite elements in Camus' work which would seem to link him closely with it. There is his preference for dealing with the existing individual and his struggles over pale and coercive systems of any kind. This deep sympathy with the living and concrete individual was at the bottom of his break with Sartre in 1952. Sartre at that time was willing to co-operate with communism for the purpose of common action. But the goal of a future, supposedly ideally just society did not in Camus' judgment justify suffering inflicted upon people living at present. (One of the controversial questions was the justification of forced labor camps in a revolutionary society.)

When Camus insists that all human life is a life led in exile, that man is a stranger in his world, the connection with existentialism seems even clearer. But Camus is quite correct in his insistence on a dividing line. The whole development of his work tended to lead him away from rather than closer to existentialism. Central to his thought is the experience and the idea of the Absurd. At its beginning stands the awesome human experience of awakening to the fact that man's comfortable world gives no answer to his question: "Why?" What is the meaning of all of this? From that moment on man is deeply and inexorably involved in the drama of the Absurd, an irrational world confronting man in which he grasps at whatever seems likely to yield clarity. In dealing with this situation, which could well be the point of departure for an existentialist philosophy or literary work, Camus parts company with the existentialists. To leap into any state of certainty—no matter how agonizingly and inwardly fought for, but detached from God, even if held only temporarily—is philosophical suicide. The Absurd must stay absurd. However since man must somehow live meaningfully, even Camus had to suggest ways of doing so. In his early work Camus tries to come to grips with the Absurd by enjoining man to be like Sisyphus. This mythic hero had been condemned by the gods to roll a huge stone up to the brow of a hill, only to have it topple back to the bottom. Though there is clearly no hope for Sisyphus ever to leave Tartarus, he still continues to move the stone. Since the Absurd, too, can never be conquered by man the stubborn pride which makes Sisyphus go on despite apparent hopelessness is suggested as the proper attitude for man.

Camus has not stayed with this answer. In *The Plague* (1947) the heroic but purely negative stubborness of Sisyphus gave way to a more positive concern with suffering mankind and a new attitude toward the Absurd. Now man is encouraged to take sides in this world against all its destructive forces. Camus soon expressed himself more specifically by equating the ideologists of all shades and the utopians of all kind, in short all extremists and dreamers of the "last great revolution," with the forces of destruction. Against them he puts the man of the revolt, who protests against any tyranny, against ideologies which dull men's minds, and against all those who want to restrict man because they think it necessary either for the improvement of mankind or just for their own advantage. The revolutionaries and extremists do not know moderation. They are far removed from the Mediterranean spirit of reason and restraint exemplified in the rebel, the man of the revolt without utopian hopes and coercive tendencies. For his own answer to the question posed by the experience of the Absurd, Camus thus would choose as his guides the Greek philosophers rather than Kierkegaard. Where the latter calls for a total abandonment Camus hesitates to follow him. There is no idea to which he wants man to abandon himself totally. Behind such an attitude Camus sees lurking the spirit of extremism. The rebel pits against it tolerance, search, and classical restraint. The ideal man of Camus puts some distance between himself and his world, not in the neutral and disinterested sense of Descartes and his successors, but in order never to forget in his state of involvement the limits placed upon man by nature. It is these limits, especially the "sunny Mediterranean heritage," which become the measure of things with Camus. This is a valid choice, since Camus denies God and does distrust man because of his dreams and fanaticism, a choice which in turn separates him from existentialists both secular and religious by its nature and implications. That in his novel *The Fall* (1957) he began to probe the problem of evil tends to show that the quest after an answer was far from stilled in him when he died in a most senseless way.

3. KARL JASPERS: MAN—JOURNEY WITHOUT ARRIVAL

The life of Karl Jaspers (born in 1883) was securely rooted in the academic soil of two European universities, Heidelberg and Basel. There was a break, however, when during the war years Hitler barred Jaspers from lecturing. The real drama of Jaspers' life was intellectual. Working first in the fields of psychology and psychiatry he soon became deeply involved in philosophy and history. After completing important works in the area of his first choice, Jaspers published the exciting and thought provoking *Man in the Modern Age* (*Die geistige Situation der Zeit*, 1931). In it he not only spells out a good many of the existentialist reservations concerning developments in Europe, but (in part IV) he devotes a whole section to what he calls existential philosophy. He thus becomes the first philosopher to use this term in the most recent connotation. From then on Jaspers brought forth a rich harvest. There is room to mention only the three volumes of *Philosophy*; *Reason and Existence* (1935), *Nietzsche* (1936), *Descartes* (1937); the first volume of his *Logic* (1947); *The Philosophical Faith* (1948); *Origin and Aims of History* (1949). It is characteristic of Jaspers that none of these is a basic book in the sense of Heidegger's *Sein und Zeit*. Taken as a whole they represent Jaspers' thinking at its best.

There is less tendency to aloofness in Jaspers than in Heidegger, but also less spirit of involvement than in Sartre. Especially since World War II, Jaspers has not shied away from a direct word on and for his time. Yet it is certain that he considers his major contribution to lie in the field of the perennial philosophical dialogue.

Heidegger's language in itself gives an impression of the man. It has the impact of a medieval woodcut, at once powerful and simple. It evokes the image of a European peasant who, his family having been wedded to his soil for generations, seems to communicate with it in all he does. Jaspers, on the other hand, has the sophistication and delicacy of an etching, although he, too, at times can speak in slow and heavily rolling sentences. He is nevertheless more urbane and polished. His life's journey through a wide section of the intellectual field has left ineradicable marks. In him the historian and the psycho-pathologist are never completely absent. It is characteristic that the work of his in which the word *Existenz* (existence) is used for the first time in its new implication should have been called *Die geistige Situation der Zeit* (1931) *(Man in the Modern Age)*. As a whole it is an essay concerned with the problem of man's life in a mass culture, and with the means by which man in such a culture can again become a genuine self. It diagnoses man's "sickness" of submission to seemingly inescapable conformity, and offers the first indication of a possible remedy. This appears in the celebrated section on existential philosophy. "Existential philosophy is that mode of thinking which utilizes but goes beyond the sciences and in which man longs to become himself. This mode of thinking does not merely focus on objects but illuminates and brings to bear the thinker's own being. Brought into flux through the transcending of all knowledge which pretends to have found the absolute (philosophical world orientation) it appeals to man's freedom (as clarification of existence) and creates the possibility of absolute actions by its constant reference to transcendence (as metaphysics)."[7]

On first reading this probably sounds baffling, but a fuller knowledge of the philosophy of Jaspers will show that it is a fairly precise statement of his standpoint. Further elaboration includes such tenets of his thinking as: the impossibility of putting existential philosophy into a final form; insistence on communication as the core of becoming truly man; the bottomless character of knowledge which requires an endless process of clarification.

Man and his journey: In Jaspers, as in Kierkegaard and Nietzsche, the term existence clearly points toward the hope for a truly human answer to the baffling problems of human life. It will not be an answer which man can just memorize and view as an object of intellectual existence. It will be one which he can make his own only by living it. In fact, even the questioning must be an existential questioning which involves man as an entity, unique and of absolute quality. And nobody has made it clearer than Jaspers that the questioning is just as close to the mystery of human life as is the answer itself. His whole philosophy is one constant reassessment, gaining a standpoint and overcoming it, never ceasing to project oneself beyond what fills one's life at the moment. Man must be like a traveler on a never-ending journey in which the horizon of today is the aim for tomorrow. He never gives up in disillusionment and despair, and never builds a shelter in which he plans to stay forever. He is at home at each day's destination, but his heart is filled with the expectations of tomorrow's horizon. Yet, as will be shown, Jaspers is no mere relativist or skeptic. The intrinsic meaning of his work is the clarification of the method, the stages, and the horizons of the journey.

Jaspers in good existentialist fashion begins with man as stranger to himself and to his world. The I, the actual man of flesh and blood asking the all-important question "who am I," is suspended between his past and his future, neither of which is clear in its totality and in its implications. The past, though already lived through, is nevertheless not wholly known to man. Much of it remains obscure. The future, impenetrable, cannot yet reveal itself since man's own future actions partially mold it. The only thing certain is that all I experience is in a state of flux and I am in the midst of it. And the world? It is no less a puzzle. If man were to shed his naive trust in harmony and in comfortable partial knowledge, he would realize that he is a stranger in the world. Jaspers joins those who deny that there can be any escape from this situation. Not to get involved in the world is impossible, since man is interdependent with his world, not a mere curious observer of it. His emphasis on the mystery of the world does not mean that Jaspers agrees with Sartre's philosophy, which sets man up as the giver of meaning to a supposedly meaningless universe. The strangeness of the world becomes for Jaspers a coded message which man receives. Obviously a message must come from somewhere. Therefore ultimately Jaspers' philosophy is a search for this center or better this last horizon encompassing all others, which makes itself known through its ciphered messages. It may be well to point out here that Jaspers uses three terms to connote this last horizon without too strictly differentiating them: the widest term is encompassing; being-as-such is used mostly when he speaks of the encompassing as the aim of thought; transcendence he uses when man's personal experience is directed toward the encompassing.

Right and wrong ways of human search for the encompassing. Man throughout the centuries has gone various ways in his search for this horizon. The history of philosophy shows a multitude of such attempts to find this "being in itself, that is that being which makes all beings an entity, is their common ground and out of which all beings come."[8] Plato had proclaimed it to be the ideas of which the phenomena of this world are imperfect images, mere shadows. After him the discussion went on until in early modern times the naive trust in man's ability to find the absolute began to be doubted. Descartes introduced a new point of certainty: *cogito ergo sum* (I think therefore I am). Philosophy came to be the confrontation of the point of certainty, consciousness, with a problematic world. The discussion continued, with the schools of objectivism stressing the world and those of subjectivism the consciousness. The skepticism of David Hume seemed to end all meaningful discussion until Kant rescued a region of possible knowledge.

This centuries-old dichotomy Jaspers hopes to overcome in his discussion of the *Subjekt-Objekt Spaltung*. (The seemingly hopeless dichotomy between the subject [the thinker] and the object of thinking.) Whenever man thinks, he is directing his mind toward something which is not himself. Even when he thinks about himself, he does not comprehend himself in his entity. Instead he makes an object out of himself and grasps only aspects of himself. Man therefore cannot think without an object and in thinking he is condemned always to go "outside" of himself for the object. The point of unity between object and subject necessarily eludes him. The material and the process which could weld together subject and object just is not available to man. That is why all the traditional schools of metaphysics have failed. They found being in itself in an object, whereas it must be sought at the point where subject and object alike have their roots. Jaspers, who prefers to think in spatial terms, calls this region of unity the encompassing, by which he refers to that last horizon which includes everything, but which itself as a whole can never become an object for man. All that is, is encompassed by the last horizon, and in any act of thinking a particular mode of this encompassing (the subject) meets another of its manifestations (object). Man will, therefore, necessarily fail in his attempts to perceive being-as-such as an object since it and he himself alike stand in the encompassing. This, by never being an object of perception can, therefore, not be defined in concepts. Only the existential thinker will be able to become aware and certain of it in particular moments. The unalterable separation of the subject from the object is, therefore, not a mere technical difficulty to be overcome by some stroke of genius or even by a little trick. It is the deepest expression of the encompassing always to show itself in some of its aspects (or modes) while keeping itself shrouded in mystery. To recall the image of the traveler, he will never reach this last horizon but all of his journey will be directed toward it.

An approach to the encompassing will be able to proceed principally along two ways. One leads through the world of objects and aims, in Jaspers' terms the "encompassing as being-as-such." Traditional philosophy chose it almost exclusively and ended by equating being-as-such with some basic substance, process, etc. found in nature and then declared to be the key to the mystery of this world. Jaspers, of course, rejects such an easy solution to the problem of ultimate knowledge. Whenever he deals with "world" and "transcendence" as the two modes of the "encompassing as being-as-such," he has no such illusions. His analysis remains wholly linked to his second way:

The "encompassing which we are." (Empirical existence, consciousness as such, spirit.) The second is the way through man; to be more exact, the way directed to and leading through the "encompassing which we are." It should not be forgotten that for Jaspers, too, man is a unique being who can overcome the sphere of mere objects and is capable of hearing the call of transcendence. Jaspers suggests three modes of the "encompassing which we are." There is, first, plain factual living as a human being (empirical existence). This means life as it is lived in its totality at every moment. It is the fundamental fact for all of philosophy that each man, including each philosopher, is an existent. This empirical existence is an entity. In the moment man tries to dissect and analyze this life it falls apart, and instead of an entity man holds in his hands mere aspects like the human body, life, or soul. The possibility of such an analysis, of course, presupposes consciousness as a new element. At first consciousness appears to belong to each separate entity, the I, exclusively; everybody his own consciousness, as it were. It makes man aware of his separation from all other objects, and unfortunately often seduces him to stay on this level and view the world from there. Those who do so end up with a world explanation tailored carefully to the capacity of their individual consciousness. The result is a radical relativism. But Jaspers looks beyond this to find consciousness-as-such, the second mode of the encompassing which we are. Individual consciousness tends to emphasize separation and makes truth not yet possible. In contrast to it consciousness-as-such is not embedded in the purely individual life. Consciousness-as-such transcends my own existence. It spans across individuals and thus creates the basis for a standard of right and wrong, in short for truth. Logic, for example, has its locus in consciousness-as-such and not in the purely individual consciousness.

Is consciousness-as-such then the last of the horizons, the modes of encompassing which we are? With empirical existence wedded to time, and consciousness-as-such the timeless place of truth, the manner of their connection seems puzzling. To establish the connection Jaspers introduces the third mode, the spirit. Though remaining somewhat vague in Jaspers' writing, spirit is best understood as the enlivening spark which brings the in itself sterile consciousness to life in the individual existence. Jaspers definitely does not, like the idealist, think of spirit as a force outside of man's empirical existence. To borrow a comparison from the field of chemistry, spirit might be called a catalyst, an agent which enables a process to happen. Spirit accounts for the historical creations in art, literature, law, philosophy, and the social order. It alone changes these creations from mere potentiality into actualities. In doing so spirit transcends both mere empirical existence and consciousness-as-such. But in the end it, too, fails to remain self-contained, and in the failure of its creation to last forever, spirit points beyond itself. In all of Jaspers' analysis of man can be seen his tendency to view man and the world in an image of concentric circles (i.e., circles in which the larger always includes the smaller). In Jaspers' thought one entity grows beyond the other by encompassing it.

The encompassing which is being-as-such. (World and Transcendence.) Is man so far analyzed the ultimate entity? Is he identical with being-as-such? Quite clearly not. "Rather this encompassing which I am and know as empirical existence, consciousness-as-such and spirit, is not conceivable in itself but refers beyond itself."[9] Man participates in the encompassing which is being-as-such but is not himself. This being-as-such is the source and aim of all our questioning. Our participation in it we have seen. As that "outside" of us we confront it in two ways. First there is the "world" in which being-as-such shows itself in innumerable ways and which has reality quite independently of our thought process. And second there is "transcendence." The two modes, world and transcendence, are closely linked to each other. Transcendence broadcasts these strange messages which we then receive and call our world. The world is not an illusion as in other philosophies, but the only language through which transcendence can speak to man. Far from having seen it this way, man has all along tried to view the world as ultimate in itself. He has pictured it as a world machine (mechanism) or as a super-organism (biologism), as chaos or self-sufficient harmony. In any case, he has refused to see the world as a message but has treated it as an answer in itself. Some particular observation about the world has been taken and blown up to a full-fledged world explanation. The results have been glittering systematic images of the world with their tragic deficiency of omitting reference to transcendence. Man, the traveler, has ended his journey within a horizon which was not the ultimate one.

When Jaspers speaks of transcendence he refers to what has above been called the encompassing. While it cannot be objectified in any way, man can encounter it as God. Is he, therefore, a pantheist in whose mind God merges himself into the world? No, Jaspers sees in the world a cipher of transcendence and not transcendence itself. Transcendence is "outside" of man and the world. It encompasses both. If Jaspers could be classified at all it would have to be as a theist.

To approach absolute transcendence, which will never be wholly known, is a purely individual endeavor accompanied by agonizing doubts and despair. Its course is the same as that which man must choose when he aims at authentic existence, which Jaspers calls *Existenz.* "Only as *Existenz* is man related to God—the transcendence—and this by means of the language of objects which reveal it in ciphers and symbols."[10] Examined more closely Jaspers' term cipher has actually a double meaning. It implies transcendence as it speaks to man through all of his life experiences. In this sense every human experience, from the beauty of a summer day to the intricacies of nuclear physics or world history, spells out the mystery of transcendence. But the term also assumes a secondary meaning. The reality which challenges man continuously leads him to interpret it. He speaks about transcendence in his own language. He invents symbols which unite his experiences and his interpretations of the ciphers of transcendence, an endeavor which of necessity must fail. By virtue of just approaching transcendence but not being able completely to exhaust its meaning these symbols themselves assume the character of a cipher.

Many have all along chosen to ignore the ciphers in the first sense, namely as the messages beamed directly to them by transcendence. They have also not escaped the pitfalls inherent in the ciphers in the second connotation. As a matter of fact with regard to them man has made some of his gravest mistakes. Instead of understanding these secondary ciphers for what they are, namely pointers in the direction of transcendence, man has integrated them as pieces of absolute knowledge into systems of faith or of philosophical metaphysics. Religious prophets, for example, have made their particular experience of transcendence, gained through their reading of the primary ciphers, into easily grasped bodies of religious knowledge. In the case of Jesus of Nazareth the attempt has even been made not only to see in how he lived and what he said a message (cipher) of transcendence but to identify him with transcendence itself as the Transcendent. Upon this tragic error churches have established their respective orthodoxies and enforced obedience to them. The challenge to an ever-renewed reading of the primary ciphers by every individual has been forgotten, or even declared to be undesirable. The metaphysicians, in their turn forgetting that God is more than just another object of a disinterested search, have built their fascinating systems which supposedly offer absolute knowledge of transcendence.

In this category belong, for example, the so-called proofs of God which through a variety of arguments seek to establish God's existence as a certainty. This resembles the procedure of the chemist who in the process of experimenting has finally obtained the substance he was looking for in the test tube. But Jaspers denies that God can be isolated, looked at, and then believed in. Transcendence encompasses everything and therefore can never be surveyed as a whole. "God is not an object of knowledge; he is not provable in the way that everyone would feel coerced to accept him."[11] The proofs of God aid in man's endeavor to discover God, but do no more. To read the ciphers of transcendence is a highly personal venture in interpretation which has no resemblance to logical proof.

Today the great metaphysical systems of the past can themselves be no more than ciphers. They are a monument to man's heroic but vain struggle to put into seemingly imposing systems of thought what can neither be totally comprehended nor clearly said. Modern man, disillusioned as he is with all metaphysical systems, lacks the naiveté to construct new ones. A creative metaphysics is no longer within the reach of modern man. All that is left to him is to reinterpret the old metaphysical systems as witnesses of past readings of the primary ciphers. This is not to be regretted, since each such system can only be a great obstacle to what Jaspers considers the right relationship to transcendence, the immediacy of reference to it at every moment of life. What Jaspers is trying to indicate here is both the positive and the negative consequences of metaphysical or religious traditions. On the one hand man, as an historical being, finds in them a source of inspiration for his own reading of the ciphers, but on the other hand he is too often tempted to forget his own reading or to hold fast to the traditions until the end of his life. Consequently the fact must be faced that in the selfhood any interpretation of transcendence held at a given moment fails in the end and becomes in itself one of the ciphers of transcendence. This ever renewed projecting of himself toward transcendence is man's destiny. It also reveals one of the great motivating forces in Jaspers' philosophy, which is to find a philosophy which combines inwardness and true commitment with a never abandoned openness to change and a readiness for re-evaluation. It is this projecting which brings up a discussion of what Jaspers calls *Existenz.*

Existenz (authentic existence). Only in authentic existence does all that has until now seemed to be an analysis of the cosmos in nearly traditional style come together into a new, a living unity. Up to this point in the discussion Jaspers could be seen as merely another observer of the cosmic scene, who brilliantly but without involvement surveys the cosmic horizons. But here Jaspers introduces into his philosophy a new center which alters this impression. Not that in an ultimate sense it becomes more important than the encompassing, the all-inclusive horizon. As a matter of fact, it does not even bring a new horizon into the picture. The concept which enters here has no clear definition. One can search all of Jaspers' writing and still not find such a definition. This is because in the strictest sense *Existenz* is no longer a category in which the life of each of us is only a particular example. Here the modes of the encompassing have found a particular and actually existing unique configuration. Authentic existence is when we become, in the Nietzschean sense, "what we are." *Existenz,* thus goes beyond mere empirical existence. In the latter we are ruled by the given, that which we are without any effort of our own by virtue of just being born and living in a given situation. *Existenz* also implies more than consciousness-as-such. With reference to transcendence, consciousness-as-such thinks, rejects, and accepts. It waives and affirms or rejects, but lacks involvement as the decisive element.

Even the third mode of the encompassing-which-we-are, the so impressively powerful spirit, cannot absorb authentic existence into itself. In spirit the creative spark aims to create entities. But *Existenz* is never finished, can never be put together with other *Existenzen* into an entity, and is in its loneliness and uniqueness absolutely wedded to temporality. While a man's whole culture in all its aspects may be impressive and look like a work hewn out of solid rock, his existence does not derive meaning from this. In *Existenz* something happens which is startlingly new. Living man, who thinks and creates, experiences in authentic existence that which he can be. He sees himself as that particular being who by virtue of free and irrevocable decisions can grow beyond the given into a real self, which in a true sense can say "I am" because it is actually irreplaceable. *Existenz* as authentic existence cannot be comprehended by psychology or logic. Some further light can be shed on *Existenz* by the following example. Obviously most persons mature in the course of their lives. But this slowly maturing into individuality is not what *Existenz* implies. *Existenz* is not a slow growth but rather a focusing of the whole person in moments of absolute and lonely decision. The unique person does not appear by natural means. In the course of conscious and free acts man becomes a re-creation beyond what he was before, he becomes *Existenz.*

How to become an Existenz? How can one "teach" *Existenz* if it is so unique that no one *Existenz* has the same content as another? The problem, of course, is one which Kierkegaard has already faced. Jaspers' answer is identical: to bring man to the brink from which he starts on his own in the direction desired. One possibility is to guide a person to the limits of what scientific thinking can do and then let him confront the darkness stretching out from there. Another possibility is the use of what Jaspers calls "existential signs," like the term *Existenz* itself, freedom, etc. If these are taken as sparks from which the individual receives the initial impulse to fulfill his life, they have served their purpose. The danger is, however, that man will take these signs as bits of general knowledge to be acquired without further consequences. The third and probably the most fruitful way, Jaspers calls the "appeal" to man to become *Existenz.* It happens when man experiences himself in his freedom, a glorious but also a frightening freedom, since there are no clear directional signs to tell him where to go. This he realizes when he is called upon to make decisions of overwhelming weight, as, for example, with regard to his religion, or when he experiences those situations which Jaspers emphasizes so much and calls the *Grenzsituationen* (that is situations into which man is placed without his choice and in which the contingency of his life, and through it nothingness, stares him in the face). These fundamental situations like death, suffering, and guilt, are just there. Man cannot penetrate through their wall of silence. He may have read seemingly brilliant systematic explanations for them. But once involved in these situations he is only a lonely individual who "has to go it alone" in the sense that the decisions he makes as to how to face these situations are his own and only his own.

In the face of the "appeal" man can choose to accept some of the philosophical or religious systems and, thus, gain new confidence. He can also act as if he had not heard the appeal and live as the daily changing situation seems to demand. Or he can become a nihilist declaring everything to be senseless. But these attitudes are a denial of the possibility and challenge so clearly present at this point to become *Existenz.* Not to respond to the challenge but to lead a life lacking authenticity is to stay estranged from what one can be and from transcendence, the supreme reference of human life. *Existenz* does not come about by itself nor will a purely intellectual, sentimental, or instinctive effort be sufficient. To become *Existenz* always requires a decision involving all of man's personality and a consequent leap into it. Man risks his whole life on such decisions taken in a puzzling world. *Existenz* never becomes a possession but remains a possibility made actual only by a constant effort. In the course of it, beside the promising hope that I can win myself stands despair over the ever-present danger of losing myself. This despair in its turn is a strong force guiding man back to his great existential task: to become an *Existenz.* A "becoming" it is, rather than a "being," since being implies too much permanence. *Existenz,* thus, has nothing to do with what external circumstances pressure man to do. *Existenz* is an internal occurrence. Since it is pulsating life at its fullest, and with the character of an entity, it can never be defined but only lived. Man knows himself to be *Existenz* when he experiences himself as a certainty and his life as one marked by authenticity. He can therefore live as *Existenz* even though it itself cannot be defined. Hence it becomes true that man is more than he knows about himself.

Existenz and God. Quite obviously freedom is the absolute presupposition for *Existenz.* Freedom alone opens the door to man's being what he decides to be rather than being what circumstances choose to make him. But is his freedom the same as that of Sartre, demanding that man be the creator of meaning in a meaningless world? Clearly not, if one remembers that Jaspers' universe is organized in horizons of which transcendence, which we here can call God, is the ultimate one. In freedom as *Existenz* man becomes aware of God as never before. Freedom reveals itself as a gift from somewhere beyond itself. Freedom without God only leads to man's searching for a substitute God closer to himself. Usually he himself tries to become God. Then freedom results in being the mere stubborn persistence in his own acts in the face of a world which is a void. Freedom and God are inseparably linked: freedom without God is arbitrariness; only God can offer that point of reference to which *Existenz* in freedom can turn without being cut down in its scope and still be more than mere desperate insistence on man's own value. The God who is not experienced in the freedom of one's own *Existenz* is the depersonalized God studied in books. At this point one is reminded of Kierkegaard, except that the strictly Christian interpretation is dropped, while the encounter with God is left at the core of *Existenz.* A meticulous observer may also object that Kierkegaard's God is the totally other, while Jaspers' God as the last horizon is remote but still somehow akin to man, since they meet in the primordial unity of subject and object, in the encompassing.

Vernunft and Existenz. Lest it should be thought that what Jaspers is aiming at is primarily a self-created attitude which once gained is held fast in later years, the important concept of *Vernunft* should be mentioned here. In English there is only the word "reason" to translate the two German words *Vernunft* and *Verstand*. The latter Jaspers interprets as that aspect of reason which grasps objects, tries to make them intelligible by concepts, and is a part of consciousness-as-such. *Verstand* is thus the tendency of reason to put man at ease as a knower. It gives him the satisfaction of at least having mastered parts of his world. *Vernunft*, however, grips the total person, not with a feeling of possessing knowledge, but with a continuous dissatisfaction with the known. *Vernunft*, this relentless force of never being satisfied with his answers, pushes man "beyond," through all the horizons to the ultimate one. In doing this it offers the everlasting challenge of doubt and stimulates the never ending search for truth. It necessarily and continuously challenges *Existenz* as the truth man lives, that which has his wholehearted affirmation. *Vernunft* and *Existenz* together form man, so deeply split and still so impressively fused, the one driving to ever new vistas and the other taking hold of truth with the whole of man's being. "Thus *Vernunft* and *Existenz* are not two opposed powers which struggle with one another for victory. Each exists only through the other. They mutually develop one another and through one another find clarity and reality."[12]

Communication of Existenzen. *Existenz* is not a solitary endeavor in the sense that it can be lived in isolation. The necessity for living with others implied here has, however, nothing in common with the utilitarian view of the benefits of social life for survival. Instead Jaspers refers to the seeming paradox that while man chooses authentic existence alone and for himself and arrives at a point of certainty, he always is immediately confronted with another opinion, faith or view. Absolute claim stands against absolute claim. Exactly the communication needed to bridge the wide open gulf appearing in this case is that suggested by Jaspers. In such a communication man no longer wants to bring his opponent to conform. His arguments aim not at victory but at coming closer together in common human concern. The struggle ensuing will be a "loving struggle" between two *Existenzen*. Its result, if this term can be used at all, is the common search after and the common experience of truth, lived and fulfilled. Every genuine truth tends to communication not to isolation. For that reason communication is at the very core of true philosophy.

Ultimate failure of Existenz. Yet however much *Existenz* lifts man into his truly human place, central as it is in that historical locus in which all the horizons of the encompassing become visible and at the same time gain perspective, *Existenz* (authentic existence) fails ultimately. Its failure cannot be avoided by technical refinement or clever manipulation. The failure of *Existenz* makes clear that man will never be able to solve the mystery of his existence, not even in the most individual and authentic attempts. Human freedom meets its limitations in terminal situations, especially death. At this point man becomes aware of the non-being of all beings. *Existenz* is marked by an endless striving and there it likewise ends. Success is not even possible, because it would imply a self-sufficiency in man which the very reference to transcendence excludes. A comparison with Goethe's *Faust* is instructive here. He, too, was striving, but in the end there is a decisive difference. Faust had become dissatisfied with all knowledge. He wanted "the" great satisfaction, which like bliss would fill his life with meaning. He finally finds it when he hears the sound of work being done to gain land from the sea. Jaspers' *Existenz* resembles Faust in his striving and longing. But Jaspers' man knows that the moment of finally embracing meaning will be forever withheld from him. Striving, momentarily filling a cipher of transcendence with meaning and then striving again is his lot. A voluntarily chosen lot, it should be added, since nobody is forced to lead an authentic existence. The question may arise whether this is not the same striving without end and meaning to which Sartre's man is "condemned." That it is not, will be seen if one follows Jaspers one more step in his interpretation of the ultimate failure of even *Existenz.* This failure likewise is interpreted as a cipher of transcendence, the supreme and perhaps the hardest for man to accept. But there is also hope. While unauthentic existence, letting oneself be driven or fulfilled from the "outside" fails and leads to despair, there is hope in the very failure of *Existenz.* In this failure the radical openness of man toward transcendence is irrevisibly expressed. This view has been likened to the heroic pessimism of Unamuno. As long as the word pessimism is in both cases not equated with hopelessness, there is no objection to such a classification. Critics have kept hammering away at Jaspers' insistence that man goes on and on in his search. They have generally doubted that man can live without a definite answer spelled out unequivocally. Man, for them, must rest in some place to feel security and direction. An attempt to answer this seeming dilemma will be made at a later point.

There remain still a few specific problems. What about the alleged irrationalism of the philosophy of Jaspers? What is the meaning of history, if we accept his interpretation of life? And after the rejection of all creeds and dogmas—what then?

Irrationalism or not? The supposed irrational character of Jaspers' philosophy is best discussed in connection with his attitude toward the sciences. For Heidegger, the scientific viewpoint is never more than a possible projection system, the function of which is left unclear. As for Jaspers, it must be remembered that during his life he had been deeply involved in creative work in some of the sciences. Consequently it is far from his mind to condemn them as worthless. In the sciences the human urge to know is manifested. Even more, Jaspers insists that they are the fountainhead of that critical thinking without which no philosophy of the twentieth century can be fruitful. The sciences, with their single-minded preoccupation with what is supposedly factual, act as the modern consciousness against dogmas, superstitions, and phantasies. They serve as the disciplinarian reaching deep into the realm of philosophy. The modern philosopher must go through the sciences and constantly refer back to them. But he must go beyond them. Scientism, as the experiment to let the sciences give the ultimate answer, is a tragic error. All sciences rest on presuppositions accepted rather than proved, arrive at probable and not certain results. Even the most celebrated results are only correct but not the truth.

Aside from this, the arbitrary limitation to one method of investigation excludes a good deal of what man's world is from even being noticed. The sciences, thus, grasp only aspects of what life is. The fullness of life escapes them, because they deliberately exclude from their endeavor the scientist as an existing person. The scientist is supposed to be the dispassionate observer. A scientific analysis of religion, for example, will be able to say meaningful things about religion. It will, however, not exhaust the religious experiences of man. Even if it came to the conclusion that "God is," this would not mean anything beyond a plain factual statement for any person who does not live his life according to the implications of this statement. The God of purely intellectual discussion remains "a God known" not a "God experienced." This grasping only of aspects of the world is the reason that the sciences in general should not attempt to give complete world views. Any such attempt leads to nothing but a new mythology. Its characters are no longer gods, demigods or demons, but matter, process, and mathematical formulas.

While Jaspers rejects such an outgrowth of scientism, he still insists that philosophy needs the sciences. They are the guides to the limits of that knowledge which can be incorporated into abstractions. Beyond these limits lies the inexhaustible world in which each step forward leads to the horizon of transcendence. In the sciences, reason as the explainer (*Verstand*) rules supreme. At their borders, reason as the doubter takes over to push man farther in the adventure toward an authentic existence. Here, in the endeavor of the philosophical world orientation (Jaspers), the limits of the sciences become even clearer in retrospect. When the philosopher deals with truth, he aims at a truth underlying rather than identical with the correctness of scientific results.

The philosophical world orientation, however, has its own dangers. Even philosophers have tried to prevent man's continuous journey farther by solving the puzzle on their ground. The positivist lets the object rule supreme over the subject, while the idealist does the opposite. Both have no sense of that all-comprehending horizon which, as the encompassing, harbors the primordial fusion of subject and object. The search beyond the limits of scientific and philosophical world orientation Jaspers calls the clarification of *Existenz*—already dealt with in the discussion of *Existenz*—with its going beyond terms, words, and the purely intellectual to the "appeal" directed toward man as entity to realize himself in *Existenz.*

While all of this shows Jaspers' attitude toward the sciences, it admittedly does not offer too clear an answer to the question: irrational or not. This is because in the end such an answer depends on the particular interpretation given to the term irrational. If a philosophy which denies that the absolute can be mapped out and described in detail is irrational then Jaspers is an irrationalist. The same is true if the permanence ascribed to insights is taken as a criterion. Jaspers denies permanence to all views. His treatment of the sciences, his insistence on the double role of reason, and the character of his own thinking show, however, that some caution must be exercised in judging Jaspers.

Philosophy of history. The second specific problem is what kind of philosophy of history may emerge from Jaspers' philosophy. Fortunately Jaspers has devoted a good segment of his work to this very question. As might be expected, Jaspers rejects any philosophy of history which suggests that events of the past, present, and future follow a rigid pattern. Both those who see history pursuing an unbending course toward ever increasing progress and those who view it as a sequence of unrelated cultures, succeeding each other and emerging and dying like flowers, pretend to know too much. In the core of their views there is a denial of the freedom of man and, thus, his possibility to choose meaningfully (see Kierkegaard's objection to Hegel). History is, however, not a chaos as this might suggest. On the contrary Jaspers himself ventures into an interpretation of world history. For him history shows four great events.

1) First comes the all-important step of becoming human in a more than biological sense when man creates his language and invents his tools and fire.

2) Out of these prehistoric times between 5000 and 3000 B.C. grow the great early civilizations of Egypt, Mesopotamia, China, and India. They share the entirely new elements of large scale organization, of writing and the clear establishment of social classes. Here also appear differences in the respective attitudes toward life, the great separating force among mankind.

3) The unity of mankind is re-emphasized during what Jaspers calls the "Axis-Time" (*Achsenzeit*). Here he refers to the fact that between 800 and 200 B.C. there appear great thinkers, secular and religious, in China, India, Palestine, Persia, and Greece. Cases in point, according to Jaspers, are: Confucius, Lao-tse, Mo Ti, the formers of the Upanishads, Buddha, the Hebrew prophets, Zoroaster, Homer, and the early Greek philosophers. What they share is an entirely new audacity to challenge the whole tradition of their respective societies. They speak out for rationality over myth and for one God or one substance against a full array of gods and demons. Theirs is an attempt to penetrate alone into the realm of being-as-such into which man earlier ventured only in the company of traditional guides. All of these men do more than just establish new views of man. Jaspers gives them the credit for having made man what he still is today. All of man's

thinking still moves within the area staked out by these thinkers.

4) And, finally, comes the scientific-technological revolution within Western culture. Its implications are not clear yet. Its consequences appear in both the achievements and the catastrophes of our time. In addition man feels almost physically how every day increasing scientific knowledge overcomes what yesterday had still been certainty.

This all adds up not to a neat pattern for explaining history, but rather to a very loose classification of what has been. What does Jaspers have to say about the future? If one can ascertain anything about it, Jaspers would be most likely to say that it will bring the increasing growing together of all historical units into one world. History will become truly world history, instead of being only a series of loosely linked local histories. And this, notwithstanding all talk of the recurence of the old, is a genuinely new factor. Quite obviously Jaspers' interpretation of history leaves the future wide open. No Golden Age is promised, no decay of cultures is prophesied, and no plan is designed according to which history must proceed. The meaning of history? It does not lie in any stage of history itself. Experience teaches us that each stage ends and is overcome. All philosophy of history stipulating an ultimate end of history in one special stage will necessarily fail, and with the impossibility of such a philosophy of history the attempt to derive from it meaning for the life of individual man fails. Man cannot be interpreted as a pioneer in or as waiting for some age of fulfillment. Neither the meaning of history nor that of individual life can be found "inside" itself. Both point to transcendence, to God. This does not reduce history to something superficial and negligible, since only as an authentic existence in an historical situation does man grasp his life's deepest meaning, and only in the perspectives of history can man gain the experience of the tremendous latitude of his own self.

A further illumination of this Jaspers gives in his treatment of the problem of the unity of mankind. Some see in it the grand goal of history—one state, one civilization, and perhaps one synthetic religion. It is not so with Jaspers. The unity of mankind is a goal with him too, but only as that condition of mankind which will enable the communication from *Existenz* to *Existenz* to proceed more freely than ever before. The unity of mankind assumes the form of a challenge to a nobler humanity rather than being a goal in itself or a panacea. The latter view would give history a meaning in itself, the former aims beyond it to the encompassing. Jaspers is not optimistic about the achievement of his kind of unity of mankind. The why hardly needs to be explained in detail to the reader who observes the contemporary scene. "Not only is naked force, lust for power, adventurous policies and the unrestrained passion for war prevalent in wide parts of the world, but there remains the still more fundamental question of whether any belief in a possible and easily achieved harmony in this world is not altogether an illusion."[13]

Again arises the decisive question: can man live according to Jaspers' philosophy? Yes, Jaspers would answer, if man shares his "philosophical faith." Its essential tenets are the God who is as the last horizon, the last reference, whom we experience as the center of our being and still is utterly far removed from us; the God who is not pictured in any particular form; who is not appealed to in prayers but through an authentic existence; the God who is not known through a single act of revelation but becomes known in the freedom of every individual life; the man who decides to live authentically, that is with reference to this horizon and unperturbed by the fact that he is unable ever to become a finished entity; in short the willingness to immerse oneself totally in a lived discourse between *Existenz* and God.

As far as Christianity is concerned Jaspers never rejects any particular religious tradition as long as it does not disrupt the individual existential experience and does not declare itself to be the exclusive truth. Against such exclusive claims for one reading of the ciphers of transcendence he writes: "We must abandon the religion of Christ, that sees God in Christ and bases the doctrine of salvation on an idea of sacrifice found in Deutero-Isaiah and applied to Christ." "No man can be God, God speaks exclusively through no man, and, what is more, his speech through every man has many meanings."[14]

C. The Religious Existentialists

The history of the relationship between philosophy and religion all through the centuries of Western intellectual development has been the history of a rivalry. Sometimes it appeared to be resolved, sometimes it erupted into outright hostility. All attempts neatly to separate the two fields of human endeavor by giving each a field of activity of its own have failed. This is inevitable, since their aim to find the truth and thus the meaning of man's life brings them face to face at their most profound level. They are made indivisible by the nature of their concern. This, as a matter of fact, has already become apparent, since none of the so-called secular existentialists has been able to avoid a discussion of God. Jaspers even says directly that for any philosopher to ignore this supreme human concern with God is either negligence or dishonesty. To do so, is, to borrow Tillich's phrase, to deny the ultimate concern of man with reality.

Thus when the existentialist current became a major influence in European thought, its penetration into the sphere of religious thought could hardly be unexpected. Especially, one must add here, since there are features in existentialist thought which facilitate bridging the gap between it and religious thought. There is the important factor that one of the great ancestors of modern existentialism was Sören Kierkegaard, a true *homo religiosus*. Consequently much of the existentialist influence on Protestantism has essentially been a Kierkegaard influence. Moreover the existentialist themes of estrangement and authentic existence could not fail to attract the attention of religious thinkers, especially since in connection with them the existentialist analysis of man has emphasized such disquieting experiences as anxiety, despair, and forlornness. To both the Christian and the Jewish tradition a philosophy like existentialism which brings the whole man and his experiences to bear on human concerns should have been a welcome development after centuries in which all aspects of man except his consciousness had been rigidly purged from the philosophical scene by most philosophers. In a sense the simple but deeply moving despair and hope of the Biblical Job have returned to philosophical questioning. Christianity, Judaism, and existentialism could be joined because at their very cores, namely their personalistic interpretations of man, they are congenial to each other. The existentialist impact on religious traditions could, furthermore, only be deepened by the historical situation following the First World War. The collapse of traditions and institutions, the destruction of much material wealth, the smothering of long cherished hopes for a Golden Age, together with the emergence of the neo-barbarism of the totalitarian regimes, provided an intense shock for a people who had even in the field of religion found a smooth routine way of doing things.

The fusion of the existentialist mode of philosophy with the various religious traditions was, however, not painlessly achieved. Existentialist influences have all along been opposed by a good many within the various religious traditions. These critics have preferred a re-emphasis on the old and traditional to the sometimes venturesome and startling innovations proposed by the existentialists. The misgivings of the traditionalists are rooted in one grave problem encountered in the process of an existentialist reinterpretation of traditional religious beliefs. Existentialism strongly emphasizes the personal search, struggle, and agony accompanying the quest for truth. It wants truth to be open to change and authentic existence to be a lifelong becoming. In addition those existentialists who like Jaspers, admit the relevance of the transcendent for man are very reluctant to affirm any specific religious tradition. Traditional religious truth seems to stress definite and unalterable commitment to one creed with all its finality. Existentialists savor the process of questioning, religious traditionalists the joy of having found answers. Religious existentialists in their reinterpretation of traditional teachings have had, therefore, to re-introduce the passionately searching "single one" into a world which had become marked by a serene certitude. Immediately, this "single one" questioning everything with the passion of his whole being came into conflict with what has been considered sanctified knowledge. In Judaism this knowledge was represented by detailed and rigid laws, in Christianity by the known act of revelation of God through Jesus of Nazareth and its many interpretations. For far too many, the acceptance of this knowledge seemed to present no particular problems. To them the existentialists put the question: must the religious endeavor center around an objective system of truth which man can only accept or reject? Can whatever is supposedly "known" not be interpreted in such a way as not to exclude the genuine journey of every man to God, alone and by himself?

It will soon become apparent how much ingenuity such a task really affords. Time and again the dynamics between the question and the answer, the searching individual and the "known" God threatens to destroy every solution found. Traditionalists of all kinds have pointed to this precariousness exhibited by all the works of the religious existentialists as a sign of weakness. It can however be more validly interpreted as the expression of the true dialectic between question and answer which cannot be eternally resolved by one answer. The religious existentialist would explain the outward solidity of all religious answers based on systems as being achieved by sacrificing the element of radical individual questioning. Even the sharpest critic of the religious existentialists will have to admit, however, that by virtue of their approach they have brought a vigor into the contemporary discussion of religious problems which had been notoriously absent for a long time. Nor is this likely to remain their main contribution. As in philosophy, no one will be able just to ignore or forget their work.

1. PAUL TILLICH: MAN—SEARCH FOR THE "NEW BEING"

Paul Tillich (born in 1886) comes from a German Protestant family. His youth was sheltered and his religious background traditional. Into this fairly tranquil life broke the First World War. It gave him a new dimension of experience which slowly transformed his outlook. He was drawn from pure theology into social and political problems. Tillich soon became one of the foremost German "religious socialists" who proposed a radical re-forming of German society. At the same time he was filling professional positions at various German universities. Of these probably the most important for his future was the professorship at Marburg on the Lahn (1924). It brought him into close contact with a group of scholars who later on were leaders in the re-shaping of German Protestantism (Bultmann and others). Heidegger also held a teaching position there at the same time. The installation of Hitler as German Chancellor proved to be a turning point in the life of Tillich as in so many other lives. Dismissed from German universities he accepted a call from Union Theological Seminary in New York (1933). The transfer from Europe to the United States brought a major shift in emphasis in Tillich's work. The socio-critical writing ceased, to be replaced by a preoccupation with theological problems. Since 1954 Tillich has taught at Harvard. His output of articles and books has been impressive, including the publication of his chief work, the *Systematic Theology*.

The balance of question and answer. Kierkegaard has undoubtedly been the greatest moving spirit in all of European Protestant thought since the First World War. His influence, however, has been inspirational rather than dominating. Consequently it can result in two theologians as different as Paul Tillich and Karl Barth. In Tillich's work, admirable as it is in scope and depth, Kierkegaard would find two features he hardly could be expected to like. One is Tillich's careful balance between the radical questioning of one's situation and its affirmative answer, faith. Kierkegaard had given up the hope that such a balance is possible. His answer was total abandonment to the paradox and the absurd. Tillich has always been too deeply involved in Western philosophical and theological tradition to do this, although abandonment in a modified sense has also been his answer. Nor would Tillich's predilection for systematic theology have appealed to Kierkegaard. As a matter of fact, it may rightfully be asked: balance, system? Does this not automatically lead Tillich outside of the existentialist circle? The answer is negative. True, a wide gulf seems to lie between Kierkegaard's contempt for all systems and Tillich's work. But this is not so if one considers Tillich's relation to Heidegger and Jaspers. Between him and these two philosophers there is a good deal of interrelationship. Not a little of it comes from the fact that both Heidegger and Jaspers are much more systematic than existentialists would be expected to be. Tillich's preference for systematic treatment is, however, as carefully restrained as it is in the two existentialist philosophers. In all of them is present the awareness of the great pitfalls in a systematic answer to human questions. In line with this Tillich makes a distinction between systems in a narrow and a wider sense. The first kind starts with a set of the highest presuppositions and deduces from them a whole hierarchy of lower ones. The second kind arrives at certain propositions, but far from building them into a pyramid of propositions, just links them together. Such a system is consistent and interdependent, but not hierarchic-deductive. In this connection Tillich makes an interesting point which sounds like a condensed "creed" of an existentialist: "Every meaningful fragment is an implicit system, as every system is an explicit fragment."[15]

Closely linked with existentialist thought also is Tillich's classification of himself as an empiricist. With existentialists in general Tillich, of course, does not mean the now predominant empiricism of the natural sciences. As the guiding principle of his empiricism he sees the starting out from one's whole life experience. Instead of insisting on the exclusive use of one method to analyze the experience, one must choose in each case a method which corresponds to the reality analyzed. For Tillich this affirmation has the additional importance of keeping a place for theology in the human quest for answers, since there is a reality which deserves the term religious and which has at its core man's ultimate concerns about reality, including his life.

It is not possible to view this ultimate concern of man with dispassionate interest? Yes, answers Tillich, but the person doing so is then not a theologian but a philosopher of religion, analyzing and describing how people throughout history have dealt with this ultimate concern. The theologian is involved or, as Sartre would say, *engagé*. He stands within one of the answers to the ultimate concern. This is not a harmful limitation of his horizon but a necessity. "The participation in a religious reality is a presupposition of all theology. You have to be within the circle of a concrete religion in order to interpret it existentially."[16] What Tillich expresses here is a paradoxical fact of life, namely that each question man asks comes from a basis, a traditional answer, on and in which he already stands. Tillich thus makes it clear that all his questions are raised in the clear recognition that he stands in the Christian tradition. He has no fear that this will impair the validity of his questioning. He sets out on the path of the existential thinker fully aware of his point of departure. "I am going to speak now about Christian Theology as the only one which is within my existential reach."[17] This is the first time we encounter the characteristic joining of existential questions with answers from the Christian tradition in Tillich's work. On the one hand, to put it into his terms, is the ultimate concern of man with reality, experienced by all man at all times and expressed in the religious symbols of all religions. On the other is the particular expression of this concern in the Christian tradition. When Tillich tries to do justice to both of them, his careful balance between the wide-open question and the particular answer has, of course, marked consequences for both sides.

As might have been expected, Tillich devotes much attention to the manner in which existential questions and religious answers are joined to each other. "Question and answer must be correlated in such a way that the religious symbol is interpreted as the adequate answer to a question implied in man's existence, and whether asked on primitive, pre-philosophical, or elaborate philosophical terms."[18] The verb correlate should be noted in this sentence, since it points out the concept important in Tillich of correlation between fundamental human questions and Christian answers. The experience of human finitude implies, thus, the idea of God, expressed in an adequate symbol. Man's existential experience of being at the end of his rational capacity refers to that which the symbol of revelation stands for. When man despairs, he implies a question which leads to the answer which is symbolized in Christ. To affirm this it is, of course, necessary that question and answer should not only be related by some arbitrary act of man, but that there is a structure which actually underlies the world. This means that man does not invent himself and his answers but finds through a radical questioning his locus within all that is. To correlate therefore is not merely a method used by man. It is a reflection of the order of things, even if, as in Tillich, this order is viewed as a field of tension. Accordingly, to analyze man's situation it will be necessary to look at man and the tensions within him which give birth to his ultimate concern. The implications in this tension will be followed to that on which the concern is focused, God. Finding that the tension, or better, dialectic between man and God leads into mysterious depths, man will then have to explore the dialectic itself. Here, if he follows Tillich, he will open the door to a centuries-old world of mediation between the human quest and what it aims at but cannot fully catch in concepts, the world of symbols.

Analysis of man. For long stretches Tillich's analysis of man runs parallel to that of Heidegger. With him, too, man's existence is rooted in the dynamic relation of being and non-being. The latter, just as in Heidegger, is not to be thought of as destroying or denying being but as a second pole. This might be illustrated by the example of the two poles of magnetism which together create a magnetic field. They are opposites but creative ones, as can be seen in the field of tension they produce. Being alone would be sterile and impermeable. Man becomes aware of this tension when he experiences non-being in his life. Facing fate in general and death absolutely, he comes to know himself as a finite being. This certitude of death is not only an interesting facet of life but grips the whole human personality. It actually makes man a human being because he is urged and becomes able to ask what it means to "be." Here in Tillich's work is another juncture of existentialist thinking and Christian tradition. Heidegger was content that man should live a life in the spirit of awareness of finitude in the "clearing of Being." Sartre takes the awareness as the indication of a meaningless world, while Jaspers understands it as a guidepost to transcendence, but one free of traditional inscriptions. Tillich drives his analysis of this human predicament considerably farther. Standing in the Christian tradition, as he does, he is forced to do so. He significantly proceeds along the well known existentialist path through the analysis of anxiety.

Anxiety, this fundamental experience of man, rooted in

man's awareness of his finitude, is the real origin of the ever-recurring question: What is the nature of man? Tillich distinguishes between an essential and an existential analysis of man. If the use of the word essential in this context should startle somebody it should be noted that Tillich's analysis of essential structures, as it turns out, is the analysis of human possibilities. It refers to what man can be since he is created in the image of God. Undeniably this essential analysis comes close to the traditional philosophical discussion of man. While the three great secular existentialists remain formal on the question of what authentic existence means, leaving to the individual existent to give it content, Tillich can be more concrete, since in the Christian tradition he can discuss the essential structure of man. This return of an essential structure of human life is of crucial importance in Tillich's work. To him, whenever possibilities enter into the realm of actualities, an estrangement ensues. Existential analysis is primarily an analysis of this estrangement of what is from its essential structures. In the case of man, this estrangement can be called the falling away from the image of God which he is potentially. Accordingly existential analysis always is directed toward and motivated by the human predicament. It is characterized by a sense of immediacy, since man himself is at stake and his whole life is always involved.

How deeply this differs from essential analysis is shown in an analysis of anxiety itself. Essentialists will see anxiety as merely one feeling among many others which are caused by a certain situation in which man finds himself at a certain time. As a matter of fact, all critics of existential analysis have said so. But anxiety, Tillich agrees with the existentialists, is, as all existential analysis views it, the fundamental experience pointing to man's estrangement. It is not just one feeling among others but an all-persuasive experience of the total person which focuses man's whole attention toward the dynamics in his structure, namely that between being and non-being. In anxiety man becomes aware of his estrangement from the image of God (or man's essential structure) he potentially is. Thus in contrast to other existentialists, Tillich takes existential anxiety as the experience immediately pointing to God. This anxiety, which is clearly no kin to neurotic anxiety, cannot be overcome by feverishly keeping busy, or by a flight from one's responsibility, be it an abandonment to abstract entities or an acceptance of ready-made answers. Nor can it be overcome in any authentic existence which remains without the certitude of God. With this insistence on the validity of existential analysis, Tillich has counterbalanced what first seemed to be an essentialist emphasis.

God. What can man express about God in words? Only one statement not symbolic in character refers to God directly: God is being-itself. This means, first, that God is the ground of all the polarity of the ontological elements without being himself subject to them. The dynamics of being and non-being, although the latter is rooted in being itself, is not present as a tension in God. But while he is not touched by it he speaks through it. As Heidegger's Being is sterile without its polar element nothingness, Tillich's God would be silent without the dynamics of being and non-being. Accordingly God speaks to man through anxiety which is expressive of estrangement (or, in other words, through man's ultimate concern with reality), a language which man can hear by virtue of his awareness of non-being (the experience of finitude). Obviously Tillich would reject the interpretation of being itself as in any way suggesting a "highest being." God must be interpreted as the power underlying all that is. To picture him as "existing" in one way or the other would make him subject to the tension of being and non-being and with it desecrate him. This is the meaning of Tillich's famous saying: "It is as atheistic to affirm the existence of God as it is to deny it."[19] Consequently any interpretation of God as first cause or supreme substance is likewise a pulling down of God to levels to which he does not belong.

Symbols. How then can man talk about God? Only in symbols, Tillich says. Therefore the symbol becomes a key in his work. Man cannot assert anything about God concretely, since in speaking he uses images out of his finite experience, in which God is not immersed in the total sense of man. When man expresses himself in his own language on the subject of God he actually does so rightly and wrongly. He is wrong since he tries to fit God into the dimensions of his finite experience. He is right since God as the ground of all being actually participates in this finite experience. Taking the symbol of "God as the father" as an example, one can clearly distinguish the two aspects of symbols. To understand the word father in its ordinary sense, as if God were in fact a benevolent parent looking down on his little children, is to fail in any comprehension of God. Making this naive transfer of a segment of empirical reality into an image of God and then insisting on its literal meaning has been the human mistake throughout the centuries. This literalism leaves unexplored the real depth of the symbol.

The case is quite different if this "God as a father" symbol is elevated out of its literal reference into the higher reality of the Holy. The symbol then is no longer secular in its nature. It refers to the relation of God and man in an empirical pattern, but with the realization that the whole God-man relation is not accurately described by it, but only one of its aspects. What has been made is not a factual statement but a symbolic one reaching into depths otherwise not touched. From the properly understood father symbol such other terms as creation, mercy, and the ground of being receive a new radiance. And in turn what might otherwise be a purely biological human fatherhood receives a new dimension by having the religious connotation added in this way. There is both dilemma and greatness in the symbol. The dilemma is that, although the symbol is directed toward the infinite, it always remains bound to the finite world from which it comes. Literalists, failing to see this, flatten the symbol into rigid statements of belief. But the greatness of the symbol lies in its participation in the reality of that for which it stands. In this way the symbol differs intrinsically from a sign, which can have arbitrary meanings. A circle, for example, can have diverse meanings if used as a sign. Whatever it "says" in a certain case is a mere matter of convention. The symbol, taken from empirical reality and participating in the reality of the Holy, can, however, be true or false. In making this assertion Tillich must defend the *analogia entis** as not being a questionable attempt to force a rational knowledge of God but man's only justification for speaking about God, if only in symbols.

As has already been indicated, the problem of truth and falsehood returns when the symbol is interpreted as being more than a sign. The latter can be incorrectly used, but it never can be false since a spelled-out convention gives it its meaning. The symbol, by referring to an actual relation between man and the reality toward which his concern is directed, can have truth. How to decide whether it is true or false is a difficult question. A symbol cannot, of course, be proved true or false by scientific methods. What then does its verification mean? "A religious symbol possesses some truth if it adequately expresses the correlation of revelation in which some person stands. A religious symbol *is* true if it adequately expresses the correlation of some person with final revelation."[20] Tillich's distinction between "possesses some" and "is" in the two sentences should be noted. This enables him to include in his view the symbols of all religions and still give a greater weight to the Christian symbols. In the one case ("possesses") the symbol is adequate only for the revelation it stands for, in the other ("is") it expresses final, true revelation.

Further to explore the implications of this connection

* *Analogia entis:* The conviction originating in medieval philosophy that the structure of God and that of the world are related in such a way as to allow man to conclude from the analysis of the world structure something about the mystery of God.

between symbol and revelation two questions should be asked: who creates the symbols, and what effect does this have on the Christian symbols? It is interesting to note that Tillich credits the collective unconscious with the creation of religious symbols, suggesting the influence of the *Tiefenpsychologie* of C. G. Jung. In a collective unconscious a primordial psychic layer out of which man's recurrent images spring plays an all-important role.

What about the Christian world of symbols? The interpretation Tillich gives to the symbol "God—father" has already been shown. He deals similarily with others. The "living" God does not, of course, mean that God lives in a biological sense but that he is the power of all life. The "personal" God has no reference to a certain person with specifically divine characteristics (like, for example, the ancient Greek gods). What is meant is that God is the basis of all that is personal and speaks to man as a person. This is necessarily so, since all existential relation is between person and person. The "fall of man" does not mean the story of Adam and Eve living at a particular time and place. What is expressed is something much more profound. Adam and Eve show man's estrangement from his essential being. Far from constituting a singular event, this estrangement is present as long as man exists. His life will always be one of estrangement because of the structure of the world. This leads directly to the new meaning which Tillich gives to the term sin. Far from being a mere violation of a set of commandments, to sin means being estranged from essential being with tragic necessity and bearing one's own personal guilt for it. This alone is sin. Original sin or any other sins would be mere corollaries of it. Consequently such symbols as judgment, punishment, and hell must be seen in the new light of man's own judgment against himself in view of his estrangement with the ensuing suffering and despair. Such a radical denial of the traditional conceptions of God sitting in judgment and of heaven and hell as actual places prepares the ground for the decisive question as to what Tillich has to say concerning Jesus of Nazareth and the revelation he stands for.

Man's hope—the New Being. In view of Tillich's position on the interpretation of what used to be traditional Christian statements of belief as symbols, it is not surprising that here again he turns against a naive literalism. Such a literalism is neither tenable in the face of scientific criticism nor even religiously acceptable, since it destroys the "dimension of depth" indicated in the New Testament. The symbol must again be the bridge between the essential and the existential, the actual and the potential. The term savior, or Christ, too, must be viewed as a symbol. Tillich rightfully points out that the symbol of a savior is not uniquely characteristic of Christianity. The man of the Stone Age already longed to obliterate his estrangement, that is to bridge that gulf which so persistently keeps essential human structure and existence from fusing. This quest, which Tillich calls the quest for the New Being, has brought man at various times to accept one or another person as the messenger through whom God supposedly speaks directly to man. Yet Tillich maintains that Jesus as the Christ is nevertheless more than just one of many savior symbols. He is that point in history in which essential structure becomes wholly transparent in existence. Man as the image of God manifests himself without disruption under actual human conditions. For once, a man appears who exists as others do but who even in his existence is not estranged from the image of God that man is. God in all his clarity shines through Jesus. Here is the ultimate revelatory situation which had never before been reached and which will never be surpassed. What man longs for in his quest for redemption had become actual in Jesus as the Christ. But although no revelation will ever go beyond that in Jesus, revelation itself will continue at all times. After all, the mystery of being itself is still with us. Even more, it still originates the ultimate concern. Every man has his own transparency, that is, he can penetrate in some of its dimensions through his own experience of estrangement. This experience is at the core of any revelation. For all men and at all times the revelation through Jesus as the Christ can be the great guide. Since the coming of Jesus, man has not been without help, although he will not feel this guide in all its necessity and impact until the ultimate concern about reality has become each person's uniquely own experience.

Authentic life is therefore more than just knowledge of a body of traditional religious creeds. It is religious existence or, as Tillich puts it, faith, because "faith is the state of being grasped by an ultimate concern,"[21] a concern not merely about an aspect of life but about the "why" of existence. Faith, although inevitably linked to doubt goes beyond mere doubt and the anxiety it produces. It affirms in the face of doubt. Christian faith asserts that "Jesus as the Christ is the concrete place where the logos [i.e., the divine self-manifestation] becomes visible."[22] The result of such an authentic existence is not to decide to join a particular denomination, not even a man who calls himself a Christian. All this is minor compared with the great experience which the man of faith wants to hold fast all his life and to communicate to others: the experience of a New Creation in the midst of the old creation of which Paul already spoke. "So if anyone is in union with Christ, he is a new being; the old state of things has passed away; there is a new state of things."[23] And if there is any one statement in Tillich's work which refers directly to his views on authenticity and the overcoming of estrangement, it is the following passage in *The New Being:* "The New Creation—this is our ultimate concern; this should be our infinite passion—the infinite passion of every human being. This matters; this alone matters ultimately. In comparison with it everything else, even religion or non-religion, even Christianity or non-Christianity matters very little—and ultimately nothing."[24]

Note on Tillich and Protestantism. Tillich's work has been used as the example for existentialist influences on Protestant thinking because of the author's prominence and originality. But his work is not the only possible example, nor have the conclusions reached by Tillich always evoked a positive response within Protestantism itself. His careful balance between the existential experience of man and the Christian tradition has not been appreciated by many of his fellow theologians. One of the most outspoken critics has been Karl Barth, who himself had once been linked to the existentialist current. He was one of the earliest and outstanding representatives of the so-called "Dialectical Theology," a current in European Protestantism in the 1920's and 1930's which was essentially an attempt to make room in man's mind for a dimension of the Holy independent from other concerns. With this went a pronounced emphasis on an individual affirmation of one's faith and a stressing of Biblical faith. The most influential ancestor of this Dialectical Theology was Sören Kierkegaard. But soon Barth parted from Kierkegaard and from all existentialist thought in general. In an interesting reversal he has since then been opposing all suggestions of re-invigorating Protestantism by the use of the existentialist analysis of man. For Barth the idea of letting man proceed through anxiety and despair to the point where he is open to and longing for his confrontation with God is as mistaken as is the idea that any ontological analysis can pave a way to God. In both cases man's ability to search and find is overrated, and God's act of grace is diminished in its glory. Only in the act of revelation through Jesus Christ is the door open to the knowledge of God, the "wholly other." Tillich's thought and that of other existentialist Protestant theologians rests on the tension between man's ultimate concern, dramatized in his anxiety and despair over his finitude, and the absolute reality about which he is concerned, God. In Barth this tension is abolished. There remains the tension, if it can be so called, of man's accepting or rejecting what God offers. But even this decision is possible only by the grace of God, since he himself makes his presence known and open for this act of choice. The same is true of the existentialist themes of despair, anxiety, disillusionment, and nothingness. They are not states of the human personality which let man discover authentic existence, but they themselves are God's work.

Existentialist themes also underlie one of the famous controversies in contemporary German Protestantism, that over de-mythologization. Beginning with an article by Rudolf K. Bultmann in 1941, this controversy centers around the question of whether or not such Biblical concepts as angels, last judgment, hell, heaven, and a glorious Messiah should not be abandoned by contemporary Christians as outdated "myths." Bultmann suggests this very cleansing process and would leave only *kerygma*, that is, the revelatory speaking of God to man in his saving act as the real message of the Bible. The Bible would then describe not factual occurrences but God's coming to man's soul and the change which this existential event brings about. This changed existence is the new meaning of redemption. In this view the Gospel is considered as a collection of myths built around the central God-man relation. In this Bultmann is a good deal more radical than Tillich, who treats the Biblical myths as symbols of the relation existing between the absolute transcendent and man. For him the challenge is reinterpretation away from literalism, for Bultmann it is complete de-mythologization. Tillich is close to Karl Jaspers, who in a sometimes very acrimonious discussion with Bultmann has insisted that the myths be treated as ciphers of the transcendent rather than being done away with as not fitting into our modern age. Since God can only speak to man in ciphers, real de-mythologization is not possible.

Others have even gone further than Bultmann. Fritz Buri calls for the taking of the last step, which is to see the whole New Testament as a symbol of each man's own existential experience. In the New Testament is given the most perfect description of the drama of man. Gone is even the central *kerygma,* the message of God in the saving act of God through Jesus Christ.

2. GABRIEL MARCEL: MAN—VENTURE IN FAITH

Gabriel Marcel's (born in 1887) family background was hardly conducive to his eventual role as one of the foremost religious existentialists. His father was the typical nineteenth-century agnostic whose truth, in the new knowledge of the social and biological sciences, knew no limit. Marcel's mother died early and her place was taken by an aunt, a Jewess with strong Protestant leanings. From her came the only religious influence on the boy. As was true for many other young French intellectuals of that periods, even more important in the forming of the young Marcel was German philosophy, especially Schelling. For him too World War I proved a shattering experience. The grim facts of war destroyed much of his liking for speculative philosophy, in which everything seems so harmoniously ordered. Man, man, and again man he now put before all phantoms of thought. Gradually, step by step, he developed into a highly personal thinker, stirred by a quest for an aim felt in a personal way and groping for an answer to fill his life. He finally experienced conversion, jubilant but serious, which led him into the Roman Catholic tradition. All that followed turned out to be an ever new penetration into what he calls the "ontological mystery." His writings, plays, articles, books, or journals all bear witness to this highly personal endeavor.

The estrangement of man from the source of his being and the means of overcoming it is the central theme of Marcel's philosophy, as it is with all existentialists. He protests against the life of modern man led on a flat surface rather than in the more valid true and full depth of human life. Modern man is seduced in two ways, by a glittering and attractive life as a functional part of his society, and by the lure of a thinker knowing only problems but not mystery. In the functional life man feels his life to be filled to the brim with meaning. We "are" teachers, husbands, wives, members of clubs, etc., etc. Our life is securely channeled in a routine but the price paid is a terrible one of de-humanization. The consequences of it are experienced in our period. Turmoil instead of the envisaged harmony and deep-reaching dissatisfaction in the place of the looked-for happiness.

Problem and ontological mystery. Tragically this neglect of what man can be is not a phenomenon encountered only among those generally indifferent to their own dimension of depth. Western culture has supplied a new, a more sophisticated life for all on the plain, in the scientific and philosophical thinking of the last few centuries. Marcel here voices the condemnation which all existentialists make of the whole philosophical development beginning with Descartes. What disturbs him, as it does the other existentialists, is the flat assertion of the *cogito* (I think) as the central fact of, as well as the point of departure for, philosophy. With it the radical separation of the subject from its object is lifted into a prominence which it does not deserve. This overemphasis does outright harm, since one of the fundamental unities of life, that between man's existence and his thinking, is destroyed. The Cartesian way of thought excludes the fullness of man's life by keeping thought out of involvement into both man's being and the world in which man stands. The purely thinking I may be compared to a weak lantern in a vast darkness. Shining just enough to penetrate a little way, it ignores the surrounding, overwhelming darkness. The Cartesian philosopher and the modern scientist are both like a man holding this lantern. He enjoys the light it gives in a limited area. Everything beyond the lantern's beam is supposedly "not yet" in the light. It is assumed that nothing still in the darkness differs radically from that already seen in the light. What is needed, according to them, is merely to increase the candle power of the lantern, that is, to go on to work patiently and improve one's method of thinking. The darkness is a barrier yet to be overcome. Thinking in problems, Marcel calls this. In his terms this thinking belongs to the realm of the "to have," the attitude of a man possessing or trying to possess an object, or even a truth, which is outside him and in which he is not wholly involved.

The ideal aim of the thinker dealing with everything as a problem is the abstract and supposedly objectively true system reflecting all objects and events in the world. What this type of thinking actually does, however, is steal away from man as he lives and establish itself in a strange and impossible independence. This thinking from a safe distance is the tragic error in the history of modern thought. Another disturbing aspect of this attitude is the implication that man must be especially schooled for penetrating into the depth of his fundamental being. Of course, if the problem were purely technical some such special training would be necessary. But the connection of man with the root of his being is a general human experience, one in which everybody is steeped. Accordingly the possibility of laying it bare is available to everybody. This does not mean that Marcel wants to do away with scientific endeavor. On the contrary, in line with the general existentialist trend he tries to show that man who is more than a functional and biological being cannot be fully grasped by a science which worships one method. The complex phenomenon, man, escapes a science which overlooks the fundamental involvement of man in his world. For the involved, the real man, thinking is more than just a tool. It is a *passage à l'être* (transition to being). In thinking, man flows into being-as-such. It opens the way to proceed to what Marcel calls the ontological mystery. It must be emphasized, however, that this is existential thinking exercised by man as he lives as an entity. Any other way of thinking finds problems but not the mystery. The difference between the two ways of thinking is not merely a matter of separating certain things which are problems from those which belong to the realm of mystery. The difference lies rather in the way of viewing things.

Marcel follows the existentialist emphasis on the "how" over the "what" in the realm of truth. Why, for example, is there so much evil in the world? Philosophers and theologians alike have been fascinated by this question and have set up many theories concerning it, as have the scientists. After reading their works one may understand what evil is. But does one actually grasp its full meaning in thinking about it as a problem detached from oneself? Definitely not. Man does so only when he himself gets involved in life and thus most probably in evil. When his personality is immersed in the complexities of evil he encounters evil no longer as a mere disturbing element in the world which interests him only theoretically. Evil has shifted from being a problem I "have" to something I "am involved in." I am challenged by it and responsible for it. Can one express more clearly that the I and the world are really not separated? If they appear separate to man first when he becomes conscious of his I, and again when he is conscious of his world, this just shows the two possible focuses of what is actually a unity. Here Marcel again stands squarely with the existentialists, all of whom hold that central to everything in human realm is the concrete, the existing individual in the here and now. Only this existing individual as a unique entity will be able to meet the ontological mystery instead of mere problems.

Problems are limitations, temporary barriers. To approach the ontological mystery does not mean to penetrate into darkness without a guide and at random but constitutes a positive and directed act. It is not an act of pure thought but rather the realization with all of a person's capacities for experience of that relation which is basic to his life and all of his knowledge. The intellect participates in this realization as intellectual intuition directed toward being-as-such. At this point Marcel plunges man into the seemingly bottomless depth of being-as-such. Any description of this venture must of necessity be far from concrete and detailed, if one can be given at all. The mystery involves us completely. Our relation to the ontological mystery can therefore only be lived not objectively known. Ontological mystery opens its doors to those who are willing to stand in it. As a part of a system of thought this ontological mystery means nothing; as the core of life it is everything.

Something which can be experienced only by the total person quite understandably cannot be brought to bear on any other person by means of teaching in flat statements. Marcel, like so many other existentialists before him, has had to choose the way of indirect communication, the appeal to man to find his own encounter with the ontological mystery. It is no mere accident that Marcel's work is so diffuse in form. It has no system of neatly organized paragraphs. Instead he offers his famous *journals* (diaries), plays, and essays. In their entirety, his works are a retracing of the steps taken in the midst of a puzzling world by a person concerned toward an authentic life. Marcel is filled by the passionate desire to bear witness to man's rooting in the ontological mystery. The specific form of his witnessing turned out to be an affirmation of one of the Christian traditions. Marcel arrives at it in a momentous experience (March 5, 1929) after years of controversy within himself. He joins the Roman Catholic Church. This joining a church with a sacramental and doctrinal structure led some people to deny him the right to be called an existentialist. They saw in the acceptance of a definite and final answer the end of any life led in the existentialist spirit. But it can be rightly pleaded that Marcel's acceptance of a faith goes far beyond the passive implication of this word. The conversion to Catholicism is responsible, however, for Marcel's rejecting the existentialist label for himself. This can be interpreted essentially as a gesture to separate his work from that of Sartre. The official Catholic condemnation of existentialism also may have been of influence, although it was directed mainly against

Sartre's type of existentialism. For those who doubt that Marcel even after his conversion has stayed within the existentialist circle, his position on human freedom, faith, and the task of philosophy should come as a re-affirmation.

Human freedom. With no existentialist thinker, not even Sartre, does human freedom infer acting in a random way according to one's purely arbitrary decisions. To define human freedom in this way shows false conceptions. Man cannot live and act as an isolated being without concern for others. Nor does he possess freedom as part of his innate equipment. Freedom means becoming in actuality what one potentially is (Nietzsche's *werde der Du bist . . .*) in a given situation. I cannot decide to become Napoleon. I am not in any way potentially Napoleon nor is my situation that of the Napoleonic time. But these limitations do not obliterate my freedom. The way from my potential I to the actual I is and remains my own and only my own. My environment is deeply and intrinsically involved in this process and is neither outside of and uninteresting to me nor does it force me to go in a certain direction. Is Marcel then a Nietzschean calling for a self-forming and creativity wherever it may lead? Of course not, because against such a view stands his affirmation of God.

Most scientific psychology fails to grasp man as a living entity and studies him as an object. It therefore cannot comprehend the full meaning of human freedom, since freedom is not a phenomenon of the surface of the human life with which it is solely concerned. Nor is freedom one faculty of man among many others. Freedom is encountered when man stands in the ontological mystery. In a striking parallel to Buber's views, Marcel considers the relationship with other persons as both a gateway to the experience of freedom and a necessity for its very emergence. Naturally this is true only if man, instead of seeing his fellowman as just another being or even a tool, builds a bridge for a genuine encounter of the I with the Thou. Freedom is realized in this meeting and in the spirit of this I-and-Thou encounter, is intimately linked to love, since only in love of his fellowman does man transcend his own limited self. The absence of love tends to isolate man, leads to distrust between man and man, and reduces their relationship to one of possessing and of being possessed. "Love gravitates toward a certain position, which is not that of my own self and not that of the other as the other; but rather toward the one which I have called the Thou."[25] And with this going beyond myself I am "open." This openness is set over against the tendency of some other existentialist thinkers either to isolate man (Kierkegaard, man open to God only) or to see human relationships as purely tragic (Sartre's stare). Man is open in an even more significant sense, namely to the *toi absolu* that is the absolute Thou.

Faith and God. The absolute Thou, God, quite characteristically emerges out of the experiences of freedom, love, and meeting. God can never be the demonstrable result of experiments or of logical operations. Such a demonstrated God would belong to the realm of the "to have." Man would know all about him and so possess him. When Marcel denies the validity of all attempts to bring God into rationally understandable forms, what becomes of the *analogia entis* so cherished in Catholic theology and philosophy? Could not God still be explained and proved by an analysis of his creation? Must there be this personal and radical encounter resisting discussion in concepts and systems? Marcel says yes, and in doing so stays in the existentialist tradition. The *analogia entis* and proofs of God have no place in his philosophy, as they are merely speculative theories. To think thus about God is to think in problems. It objectifies God, whereas God is encountered only when the total person is directed toward him. In so directing himself man does not merely recognize God in a purely cognitive sense but rather enters into an engagement with him. He becomes involved and experiences responsibility. Faith, which this engagement actually is, is therefore always personal, the encounter of the human person and God as a person. No ideology, no ideal and no abstract highest good will suffice. Relating himself to them, man will get no response. They are impersonal. The Christian who attempts to put this encounter into the form of a statement, a creed, and who sees in it a factual statement of the truth is also badly mistaken. A creed is either a challenge to become a witness for one's faith or it is a seduction to superficiality. At this point the cleavage between the traditional Thomist and the Catholic Marcel appears. Marcel is much more interested in how the concrete individual encounters God than in long abstract speculations about God or even proofs of his existence.

It is not suprising that in Marcel's work should appear the words anxiety, despair, and hopelessness. At first sight his interpretation of anxiety resembles Heidegger's. To Heidegger anxiety results from man's realization of himself being-thrown-into-the-world and of the unalterable finitude of his life. In Marcel likewise anxiety is connected with man's awareness of his finitude. But since his philosophy recognizes an encounter with God, anxiety is a state in which the human personality finds itself before this attainment or in periods of being distant from God, or, more permanently, if man shuts himself off from the ontological mystery. To oversimplify, Marcel sees anxiety as a sign of failure to open oneself to the message which God is. Anxiety can and will become despair if this openness is never achieved. A despairing man is living in a world of fate. His questions travel out into the universe but get no response. The echo which sometimes comes back (that is, the abstract theory of the universe) does not relieve his human hopelessness. Hope belongs only to a life lived in the inexhaustible ontological mystery that is love, freedom, and encounter. Accordingly it is the hope of the man who is always on his way, the *homo viator*. (Note that Marcel, although a Roman Catholic, has never written a systematic theology or philosophy.) This wayfarer to and witness for the ontological mystery represents Marcel's conception of authentic existence. It contains the "knowledge" of the existence of God wrung from the struggles of life.

But this knowledge is not a possession. Another side of authentic existence is the recurrent experience of the personal encounter with God in the actual human life with its doubts, agonies, and eventually hope and love. Any intellectual "knowledge" of God apart from that which is an integral part of authentic existence is of no importance. While man can be brought to realize where the real goal of his journey lies, actually to go there, overcoming his doubts and weariness, and avoiding the short cuts which always result in dead ends, is each man's own formidable task. Man must come to understand that a religious life (and Marcel's authentic existence definitely represents one) is the actual journey to God and not the taking of the trip on the map by learning about or establishing metaphysical or theological systems.

Philosophy? "To have" and "to be." Is there any room left for philosophy if human life is viewed in this way? There is for a type of philosophy which differs from most of modern Western philosophy. Like Kierkegaard, Marcel denies the validity of a philosophy whose glittering system of truth when once established need only be accepted as the last thing in philosophical architecture. Such a philosophy is the "philosophy of the spectator." Its strongest urge is curiosity. Man sits in a theater, fascinated by what is going on around him and trying to understand it. He acts as if the riddle of human existence could be solved in this theoretical way. All one sees is problems, whose answers belong in the category of the "to have." The knowledge gained is a possession attached to oneself like one's clothing, spectacles, or fountain pen. Its value is measured by the wideness of its acceptance. Opposed to this type of philosophy stands that of the existential thinker. It seems superfluous to repeat how deeply involved he is in his world and how interlocked his thinking is with his existence. He does not think but "it thinks in him." Only in this realm of the "to be" does man become open to the ontological mystery.

To end this discussion of Gabriel Marcel's work, we return to his theory of knowledge. The distinction between non-existential and the existential knowledge has been made abundantly clear. The first kind has as its aim sets of propositions to express objective truth. Although the non-existential philosopher may agree or disagree with these systems, as a total person he stays neutral. He is never aware that in his choice his ultimate destiny is at stake. His thinking and knowledge are purposely impersonal in order to be most widely acceptable. The creative, new and unique, escapes him. He can only grasp what is not alive and the byproducts of life. Wherever this non-existential thinking is proclaimed to be the only valid truth, it becomes outright harmful since it empties the world of all that matters. Marcel calls this the primary level of reflection. Existential knowledge, on the other hand, is personal knowledge, cast and recast in immense inner struggles of a free person. Is it then not purely subjective? Not according to Marcel, because man in his search for knowledge does not proceed at random. Aiming at the realm of transcendence he is met halfway by God actively revealing himself to man. Marcel, like Tillich, carefully strives to balance man's search with the aim of his search, God. Only through his own initiative can man come to the point where God actively reveals himself. In this secondary reflection man participates in the being which underlies everything. The subject and the object are no longer rigidly and artificially separated but are connected by virtue of participating in the same reality. Beyond the cleavage of subject and object there stands a fundamental unity. To start at the separation of subject from object is to ensure the failure of every venture in truth. Truth lies in the recalling of the unity, a recalling only possible in total personal involvement.

In the end, if it is bound to agreement at all, truth can only be the agreement of personal testimonies.

3. MARTIN BUBER: MAN—PARTICIPANT IN GOD'S DIALOGUE WITH THE WORLD

Martin Buber (born in 1878) spent his childhood in a family deeply steeped in the orthodox Judaism of Galicia which shared with most of Eastern European Judaism the richness of tradition. It also gave Buber access to Hasidism, that current in Judaism which revolts alike against empty rituals, legalism, and religious rationalism. It emphasizes the inwardness of the religious experience, piety, and humility. When the young Buber later joined Zionism it was this particular heritage which prevented him from embracing the purely political and secular Zionism. Buber has remained a religious Zionist. Studying and writing filled the years of his early maturity, culminating in the small volume *I and Thou* (1923), which contained the core and the foundation of all his writings. From 1923 to 1933 he taught at Frankfurt, Germany, and continued to publish until the era of Hitler. After having courageously offered spiritual guidance to his Jewish brethren in Frankfurt he emigrated (1938) to Palestine. Teaching at the Hebrew University he propounded a not very popular but for him characteristic policy of conciliation and understanding between Jews and Arabs. Since his retirement (1951) he has been devoting his time to educational projects. All in all his life strikes a wonderful balance between action and devotion to studies.

Philosopher on the "narrow ridge." A distinctive mark of Buber's philosophy apart from all of his ideas is the immediacy of its impact. Other philosophies build elaborate ontologies. Buber always seems to proceed to his conclusions directly from the fullness of life. Not that he is a simplifying thinker—far from it. He himself describes his way of thinking best when he says that he "does not rest on the broad uplands of a system that includes a series of sure statements about the absolute, but on a narrow rocky ridge between the gulfs where there is no sureness of expressable knowledge but the certainty of meeting what remains undisclosed."[26] To this habit of approaching the experiences of life in an immediate and ever new way can be ascribed the gripping quality of all of Buber's writings. This is the more surprising because of the wide scope and the volume of his work. On the other hand, he definitely is more systematic than Gabriel Marcel. Buber's philosophy has a very clear center from which all his ventures into the complexities of human existence start. Characteristically this core is not an impersonal being as such. Whether in the final analysis such a being is not after all the actual center of his philosophy is an interesting question. Its importance at this point of the discussion is, however, only slight, because human existence, for Buber, shows first of all a significant structure which is woven into every phenomenon connected with human life. Human existence is intrinsically a life of relationships. Buber distinguishes two such relationships in this "life in dialogue" or "dialogic life": *I-Thou; I-It.*

I-Thou. The *I-Thou* relationship, is of crucial importance. It is not necessarily the prevalent relationship, but it decides over the quality of total existence. What man becomes depends in the end on whether he is open to and standing in the *I-Thou* relationship. Only "through the *Thou* a man becomes *I.*"[27] Man emerges as a person in the sense of a whole entity solely in relation to a *Thou.* But this meeting of *I* and *Thou* is not the routine living together of human beings who unconsciously influence each other. This would be forming personality in passivity. Although this method is fashionable in the social sciences today it is far from what Buber means. What happens in the meeting of *I-Thou* is a challenge to the *I* to become truly human in a relation between two real persons. "When *Thou* is spoken, the speaker has no *thing;* he has indeed nothing. But he takes his stand in relation."[28] This does not necessarily mean that there is present in the relation a full reciprocity. A good teacher, for example, will "give more" than he "receives" in his relation with his students but the *I-Thou* character of the relation will nevertheless be preserved.

For still another reason Buber cannot be just another representative of the school which sees the self as a social product. *Thou* does not imply only man. In an even more significant connotation it refers to God. The *Thou* is thus twofold, a temporal *Thou,* fellow man, and an eternal *Thou*—God. In both cases, nevertheless, the relation *I-Thou* is deeply personal. Significantly for all of Buber's philosophy these two relations, far from excluding each other, are viewed as genuinely interdependent. Too many people of all ages have overlooked this. The mystic with his solitary sinking himself into the vast realm of God, the ascetic who flees people in order to come closer to God, even the existential Christian Kierkegaard with his preference for isolation (the "single one") all have not seen the overwhelming importance which relation to the temporal *Thou* carries for establishing that with the eternal *Thou,* God. "All real living is meeting,"[29] Buber says in *I and Thou.* It could be said that all authentic life is lived in a triadic relation: I—fellow man—God. I can only become an I, a whole self, an authentic existence, in this double relation and this is true likewise of my fellow man. As for God, even he can "live" solely through and in this relation. Characteristically Buber is speaking of the living God, not of the one merely theoretically existing. That God is not just one corner in the triangle or an equal partner in a casual conversation will be shown in the discussion of Buber's idea of God.

A further note on Buber's existentialism may be in place here. The concept of relation as central to human life implies concrete historical persons. This personal relation must, furthermore, be restored and invigorated at any given moment.

It is never complete in the sense of finality (namely, in its authenticity), but can be complete only in the involvement of man's total personality and its ever new becoming. Accordingly the "dialogical" (Buber's) man emerges as a truly existentialist conception.

I-It. While the world of the *I-Thou* is one of true personalities, that of the second relation, the *I-It*, is radically different. All *I-It* relations are intrinsically incomplete; since they are unable to fill human life with true meaning. Here man stays alone and isolated. In the *I-It* relation, I relate myself to something or even someone in a purely utilitarian and highly impersonal way. Man enters the world of tools. Genuine response is unknown in the *I-It*. Even the *I* itself remains somewhat aloof from this relation by never being able to enter it in its fullness. "The primary world *I-It* can never be spoken with the whole being."[30] Tragically, however, modern man has chosen this way of relating himself in preference to the *I-Thou* relation. All scientific or philosophical thought which is based on the strict separation of subject and object and on personal non-involvement tends to show this. "I perceive something. I am sensible of something. I imagine something. I will something. I feel something. I think something."[31] Always man is only partially involved. He never puts his whole existence at stake. He achieves a brilliant manipulation of objects but his world remains without resonance. And the malaise of the man of the twentieth century stems from this prevalence of the *I-It* and the ensuing inability to relate himself in a personal way to his fellow man and the center of his life, God.

Certain misinterpretations of the *I-It* relation must be shunned. It definitely does not stand merely for bad or evil, while the *I-Thou* implies good. If it did, Buber would be back at one of the most stubbornly maintained dualisms, that between worldliness and non-involvement in the world. It would imply that the *I-It* should be avoided. Again Buber proves himself to be a much more subtle thinker. Certainly he challenges man continuously to overcome the threat of the *I-It* dominating his life. But an avoidance of this relation is impossible by the very fact of man's involvement in his world. In the course of his life man will time and again drop from the heights of personal relation to that of the *I-It*, from the personal to the factual. "But this is the exalted melancholy of our fate, that every *Thou* in our world must become an *It*. It does not matter how exclusively present the *Thou* was in the direct relation. As soon as the relation has been worked out, or has been permeated with a means, the *Thou* becomes an object among objects."[32] This tragic destiny of man is inescapable. In order to live he must take certain steps. He must harness his surroundings to his will and manipulate them. All the elaborate arrangements to earn a living and to organize society are necessary for man's survival. And so man will time and again have to use his fellow man as a tool. "Every *Thou* in the world is by its nature fated to become a thing, or continually to re-enter into the condition of things."[33] The world is thus not evil, but a necessary part of life. The evil is letting oneself be ruled by the *I-It* relation. Then man becomes estranged from his fellow man, from God and in the deepest sense also from himself. Modern man with his preference for the mastering of the world is to Buber in this state of estrangement. The solution to this dilemma clearly lies in self-overcoming in the sense of breaking in the "open" —to the relation *I-Thou*.

Freedom. When Buber regards the overcoming of the *I-It* by the *I-Thou* relation as an everlasting task, he is, of course, referring to a man who is free. He rejects any deterministic interpretation of man. The sciences which constantly present images of the "driven" man are wrong. This man is no more than an insignificant part of a world-machine or process. Buber, like Jaspers, views the sciences as practical and useful but unable to find the whole meaning of human life. Whenever the sciences set themselves up as the last authority on truth, they are outright harmful and dangerous since they then become the main source for man's estrangement. In line with all existentialist thought Buber denies that a system can swallow up the concrete and free individual. Darwin with his biological interpretation of the world and Spengler with his historical scheme both surrendered to a fate they themselves had designed. Freedom, on the other hand, does not mean acting at random in a vacuum. The world in which we are so deeply involved cannot be made to fade away by a magic trick. To be free means to meet one's destiny and to strive continuously to establish the *I-Thou* relation and through it ever anew become a self. In this his interpretation of authentic existence Buber combines the *amor fati* of Nietzsche (the loving acceptance of one's destiny) with what he considers man's ultimate directedness toward the *Thou.* Again he is linked at this point to existentialist thought in seeing the presence in man of the polarities between what one can be and what one is, and also between authenticity and unauthenticity. Man freely makes his decisions concerning his mode of life and expresses it in his free acts.

What are the consequences of Buber's interpretation of the human condition for his concept of God, his social philosophy and his ethics?

God. Buber's image of God has already appeared as the eternal *Thou* in the discussion of the *I-Thou* relation and Buber does not go beyond this vision of God as the partner in the "human life in dialogue." This description of God as a person might lead some to conclude that God is a person and tempt them to create a new anthropomorphic graven image. But such simple imagery is far from Buber's mind. Buber asserts that God is a person only in his "dialogue" with man. His being a person in this sense is man's "door" to God. What God is, beyond what he is experienced to be in the *I-Thou* relation, is not within the reach of man's comprehension. Philosophy and theology both all too often forget this limitation. ". . . What is meant by religion is not the massive fullness of statements, concepts, and activities that one customarily describes by this name and that men sometimes long for more than for God. Religion is essentially the act of holding fast to God. And that does not mean holding fast to an image that one has made of God, nor even holding fast to the faith in God that one has conceived. It means holding fast to the existing God."[34] Buber therefore leaves open the question whether God is the *Urgrund*, that is an impersonal being out of which man and the world grow. This question seems to Buber unanswerable, perhaps even uninteresting because not relevant for man. God "as such" is a *deus absconditus* (a hidden God). The God we know is the personal one we experience in the immediacy of the "dialogue."

Consequently man can find God only in the fullness of life and in the midst of the world by relating himself to God. On the other hand such an interpretation of God as becoming visible to man only in dialogue makes possible an eclipse of God. As in a certain constellation the shadow of one planet can black out parts or the whole of another, so man can do to God. God becomes silent if he is not spoken to by man. He speaks through man and, thus, "needs" man. For the dialogue to be interrupted is the "death of God," who for man only lives in the *I-Thou* relation. The assertion that God exists despite the disruption of the relation does not change the situation. For the time of the eclipse God disappears either from the individual human life or from that of a whole group. This is a most decisive fact and one which Buber thinks is characteristic for our time.

Buber's discussion succeeds remarkably in establishing a dynamic balance between God who lives with and through man and God as a total mystery. It is hard to judge the extent to which Buber's task was easier than that of a Christian existentialist by virtue of the absence of the christological problem. Buber can preserve the immediacy of man's relation to God without having to account for the special event of the life and death of Jesus as an historical turning point in and for the life of mankind. How to proceed to the immediacy of God without somehow destroying it by some interpretation of Jesus' life as an intermediary body of knowledge which must first be mastered has proved a difficult problem for Christian existentialist thinkers.

Social philosophy. To understand Buber's social philosophy it is necessary to know about the work of the nineteenth-century German sociologist, Ferdinand Toennies. Throughout his work there is suggested a basic dualism as to the principle on which societies can be organized—*Gemeinschaft* and *Gesellschaft*. Usually these terms are translated quite incorrectly, since there are no exactly fitting English terms, as community and society. Toennies identified *Gemeinschaft* (community) with that type of society which has grown organically through generations into a unity. It is homogeneous and characterized by the natural allegiance shown to the traditionally established customs, morals, and beliefs of such a community. *Gesellschaft* (society), on the contrary, is seen as an aggregation of people living together because they find it useful to do so. The institutions of this group have been "arranged" by the members with a view to their individualistic wishes. *Gemeinschaft* or community is thus an organic unity, *Gesellschaft* or society an artificial one created by man for specific purposes.

Buber gives wholehearted approval to community as far as it implies an organic unity. Organic he would, however, interpret quite differently from Toennies, for whom it meant effortless, natural, and smooth. Buber's community, on the contrary, rests on the wholehearted co-operation of members who strive to become authentic existences. They alone can establish the true community, a form of common living diametrically opposed to the ideals of both the prevailing individualism and the collectivism of our time, both of which, according to Buber, give man no chance to develop into a person. Modern individualism with its flat hedonism, its pursuit of sensual happiness, activates some aspects of man but never the whole I. The purely mechanical association of such predominantly egoistic individuals is in the eyes of Buber the real reason for modern man's sickness and malaise. Nor is socialism, at present the most popular form of collectivism, an answer to this predicament. Instead of building man into a person, every collectivism submerges him in an amorphous, faceless mass.

In proceeding further toward his own solution, Buber introduces an additional differentiation, that between the social and the political. The social principle leads the concept of community into an even closer concordance with Buber's thought. While the early form of community showed a homogeneity produced by habits and marked by little awareness of what the individual's contribution to it must be, Buber's new community grows out of the free decision of authentic persons. The new community must be established without destroying the personal independence which man has achieved by centuries of struggle. Community must be based on the mutual recognition of the dignity of the individual person which in turn demands free persons working together in voluntary co-operation. Despite the difference between the old and the new community both represent the social principle. The tragic element of history appears in the failure of man to develop from the early community directly to its modern form. Instead he has permitted the second principle, the political, to gain predominance. The early community was assimilated into the state as the representative form of the political principle. While the social principle tends to decentralization, the political makes out of centralization a fetish. Consequently the many little groups which have emerged in the course of man's history and which have existed even within a larger community disappear before the state which demands complete and exclusive submission to it. Modern man blindly supports this demand in the hope that his salvation will come from ever larger collectives. The consequences? "The most valuable of all goods—life between man and man—gets lost in the process: autonomous relationships become meaningless, personal relationships wither, and the very spirit of man hires itself out as a functionary."[35] The human robot appears; but with him appears a paradox—an "unhappy" robot. This unhappiness shows how impossible it is for man to live as a robot, and in turn opens the door for his way out of his dilemma. Buber hopes to be the midwife to this rebirth of human togetherness in the world through his ideas and his actions.

In this great social revolution to come, power must be wrested from the political principle. Not even as a world government supposedly assuring world peace can it be condoned. World government would only be more of the same poison. The guiding maxim must be "as much as possible of all power to the small groups—the communes." Buber refers here to the groups of man's immediate experience, like the village. They are not what he would consider artificially created groups. These small communities are rather the only connection modern man still has with the age-old communities of life and work. They must be filled with a new spirit and, of course, adequately adjusted to the twentieth century. Buber's call for the rebirth of communities should not be thought to originate in nostalgia. He knows quite well that there is no way back. Nor does the new spirit refer to an emotion. It is closely linked to what has been said about the "dialogical" man, and thus includes the ideal of authentic existence with its joy, suffering, success, and failure. These new communes may submit to some necessary centralization, but only to the extent that is indispensable under the given conditions of time and place. The commune, the small unit, must remain the real center. To it Buber wants to entrust also the control of the means of production. It is for this that Buber's position has often been called "communal socialism" in contrast to the state socialism of the Marxists. While this position is important it should now be clear that Buber is concerned with more than just a redistribution of the means of production. As far as social problems are concerned, his ultimate aim remains the organized commonwealth, which "never will build itself up out of individuals, but only out of small and ever smaller communities: a nation is a community to the degree that it is a community of communities."[36]

Buber's solution carries a strongly personalistic and spiritual accent. From the author of *I and Thou* could hardly come any other answer. He himself foresaw that he would be labeled an utopian. Whether he is one or not, is a difficult decision to make. On the one hand there stand such non-utopian passages as, "Community should not be made into a principle; it too should always satisfy a situation rather than an abstraction. The realization of community, like the realization of any idea, cannot occur once and for all time; always it must be the moment's answer to the moment's question, and nothing more."[37] Through it all there appears deep and profound trust in man, a trust which is ultimately rooted in man's connection with God. On the other hand Buber's firm conviction that a communal ownership of the means of production is necessarily better than any other brings him very close to the utopians of all ages. With them he seems to sense a special congeniality between this form of economic organization and the *I-Thou* relation. So it is best to leave the definite decision as to whether Buber's ideals in the social field are utopian or not to the individual reader. The answer may well be that Buber keeps to the thin line which separates complacent acceptance of the given from the lofty ideals of the eternal utopians.

Ethics. Buber's ethical teaching is a consistent corollary to all of the foregoing ideas. His distrust of the various schools of ethics which try to catch the morally good in a formal maxim, together with his deep seated suspicion of the state, has brought people to call Buber an anarchist. Such a classification can hardly be justified, because Buber has never denied the need for social organization or even for some centralization. Nor does Buber naively proclaim that man is corrupted by his environment and would show his natural goodness if freed from social and political authority. On the contrary Buber insists that man himself has brought about his own de-humanization by letting the state become triumphant. The totalitarian regimes, for example, are only an outward expression of this fundamental fact. Against the naive declaration of man's goodness also stand man's failures, which have come from himself and not been caused by something or someone. Thus, Buber, like the other existentialists, puts the ideal of an authentic life in the center of all discussions about good and bad, right or wrong. The morally good is the actualization of what has been given man as his possibility which for Buber is the establishing of the triadic relation *I*—temporal *Thou*—eternal *Thou*. In it man lives fully, lives an authentic existence. The morally bad is the disruption of this realization in complete abandonment to the *I-It*. Once this relation becomes predominant instead of being a concession to temporary necessity, an unavoidable but still tragic one, man fails himself. He does so because he cuts himself off from his living center—God.

4. NICOLAS BERDYAEV: MAN—WITNESS FOR PRIMORDIAL FREEDOM

Very little religious consciousness pervaded the childhood home of Nicolas A. Berdyaev (1874–1948). Its atmosphere was refined and cultivated, and in it Berdyaev grew up to become a very sensitive young man. He could not stand the military academy to which he was sent in keeping with family tradition and finally ended up studying philosophy. As could hardly be otherwise in the Russia of the turn of the century, he was drawn into the student movements directed against the Czarist regime. Arrested and exiled Berdyaev became totally gripped by the great upheaval of his time. In what he stood for at that time he reflected the most diverse elements of Russian thought: Marxism, a radically rejuvenated Orthodox Church, and a love for German idealistic philosophy, mainly Schelling, whose views he combined not as an intellectual connoisseur who gathers his ideas where he can get them but as a serious man who tries hard to come to grips with a time obviously out of joint. All of these elements were grouped around Berdyaev's great and central concern, the freedom of man. It is a further indication of Berdyaev's independence of thought and action that no partisan ever accepted him. The Russian Orthodox Church started proceedings against him which were stopped only by World War I. The Communists had no use for a man who was neither a materialist nor an obedient follower of party lines (although he supported the October Revolution for its social radicalism). When he was in exile, first in Berlin and then in Paris, the Russian traditionalists shied away from him. He was again alone and far from Russia, his home. But his great inner strength enabled him to write great works and lecture widely. In the year 1948 this quite turbulent and creative life ended.

The philosophy of Nicolas Berdyaev carries the same mark of uniqueness and courageous loneliness which is so characteristic of his life. On the one hand the loneliness which he experienced in ample measure stems from his life as an exile and the fact that even there he was disliked by many of his fellow emigrants for his unorthodox views. On the other hand it was the loneliness which surrounds each pioneer who ventures new interpretations of man and his world and who in this pioneering is not afraid to be left alone on a strange path. Although both Berdyaev's life and work are marked by a never-wavering courage whenever it was necessary to be a lonely witness, he did not cut himself off from the long tradition of Western thinkers. He frequently acknowledged his deep indebtedness to Immanuel Kant, to the great German mystic of the seventeenth century, Jacob Böhme and, last but not least, to Dostoevski, Kierkegaard, Pascal, Nietzsche, and St. Augustine. The strongly existentialist bent of his philosophy is foreshadowed in this latter connection.

The dualism of spirit and objective world. To call Berdyaev's philosophy a "philosophy of freedom" is to say all and also very little. So central is freedom to Berdyaev's thought that no more fervent protagonist of it can be found in Christian thought. To establish freedom in this central place Berdyaev goes radically to work on some cherished traditional Christian concepts. This appears when he does not hesitate to do away radically with the Christian preference for a monistic explanation of man and his world. The view of the world as created and ruled by God has been held by most Christian thinkers, and dualistic views which suggested the presence of a second, predominantly evil, principle not fully overpowered by God have been constantly rejected as heretical. This makes Berdyaev's belief in a powerful dualism the more startling. On one side stands the realm of freedom or spirit, a word not to be understood in the usual sense. Spirit is freedom, creative act. Berdyaev frequently warned against interpretations of his concept of spirit in any other way, especially in a manner suggesting any sort of substance. Opposed to this realm of spirit stands the world of objects (or objectivity), the world known to man through the phenomena of his daily experiences. The bridge which connects the two realms Berdyaev calls the process of objectification. This mystery of objectification, the way the objects of our world "grow" out of the realm of the spirit, the way spirit becomes "externalized," is closely connected with Berdyaev's problem and theme of estrangement. In Kantian terms, this would have been a question of how noumena (that understood by intellectual intuition) become phenomena (things experienced through the senses).

Especially care must be taken to notice all of the asp cts

of Berdyaev's process of objectification. For him it is not a mere problem of epistemology, that is, one connected with the processes of getting knowledge. The mystery of objectification is not exhausted by diligently searching for a solution to the question of how man as a being belonging to the realm of the spirit (or freedom) can best acquire knowledge of a world of objects outside him. Such a superficial interpretation of objectification fails to note the central fact; namely, that man himself has been objectified. In living in the world of objects he has left the realm of the spirit and, thus, become estranged from his "home." This tragic event and its consequences are much more interesting and important to Berdyaev than mere epistemological problems. Berdyaev is concerned with the metaphysical problem which constitutes the process of objectification. The momentous occurrence of the spirit ejected from its own realm and injected into that external to it interests him. He wants to discuss not the thought problem posed by it but the actual separation of objects from spirit. He does this not out of mere human curiosity but because of man's vital interest in this process of objectification. By virtue of it man and his world show a real opposition between two realms, that of spirit and freedom and that of objects. "How the two stand to each other may be put in this way; appearance is the objectified world, the natural and social world of necessity, servitude, enmity and dominance; whereas the noumenal world is spirit, freedom and creative power; it is the world of love and sympathy."[38] The tragedy of much of Western thought has been that is has overlooked the "fall" (that is the alienation of the spirit from itself) which precedes the world of objects. This has made it possible for Western thought to preoccupy itself with the world of objects without ever asking for the ground out of which they grow. What was discussed were the more or less real qualities of phenomena without regard to the "fall" which precedes and underlies everything. Accordingly the necessarily evil quality of objectification was also disregarded by taking the objects as merely given, as facts, without suspicion of their evil aspects. Truth for these thinkers was a perfect knowledge about the objective world without referring to the mystery of objectification in spite of the deep involvement of man in this "fall," of spirit externalizing itself in objects. The truth these thinkers found was, therefore, never an existential truth of man grasping his being in freedom in a world of objects, but only a technical knowledge.

The dualism in man. The two realms of the cosmos, freedom and objectivity, are reflected in man's existence. Man is man only because he is deeply steeped in the realm of the spirit and freedom. This is the primordial cosmic or "meonic freedom" of Berdyaev and not the social and political freedom of liberalism, which can be expressed in various rights. It is a freedom which underlies man's whole existence as a challenge which calls him to see in freedom his highest obligation. This challenge is never ending, since actual man living in the world participates in the objective world and is constantly tempted to forget the freedom he is. Only by creative acts can man build and rebuild his personality and triumph over the world of objectification. All theories of personality which overlook this fundamental fact are false. So are the fashionable biological and psychological theories which try to see the forming of personality as exclusively happening in the realm of objectivity. By virtue of this man remains locked in a world of necessity. But personality is destroyed rather than formed there. What such a psychology sees is only the individual as a category of the natural world. Man understood as such an individual is submerged in the external. There he is subject to the conditions of necessity and causality and open to coercion by the social arrangement. The ideal of this level of existence is the average, the adjustment to that which is, and a subsequent loss of uniqueness.

Consequently Berdyaev says no to any humanism which relies on a naturalistic interpretation of man. Its historical value as a movement furthering the case of man he grants, but its failure to anchor man in the realm of the spirit he deplores. Those who stand in one of the Christian traditions should not, however, exclude themselves automatically from the ranks of those Berdyaev criticizes. He protests against the limitation of the freedom of the human personality advocated by those Christians who have a purely servile understanding of the divine-human relation and of religious life. In dealing with the divine-human relation Berdyaev follows new paths. That human personality must be linked to the divine is a direct consequence of the fact that God and man alike reside in Berdyaev's realm of the spirit. Man is created in God's image. We have spoken before, for example, of man as steeped in freedom and as the originator of free and creative acts. But do not all, even the greatest creations by man, end in failure? The cultures, the great revolutions, the empires all disappear eventually in the melting pot of history. Unlike Jaspers, who sees this failure as final, Berdyaev sees lasting results from human creations. These show not in the world of objectivity, however, but in the realm of the spirit. Berdyaev's eschatological orientation allows him to speak of these obviously tragic failures as contributions toward the Kingdom of God to come. Even this consolation does not take away from failure any of its tragic quality for man in the moment he experiences it. Still man remains a genuine contributor to the Kingdom of God, because that is not the work of God alone. This co-operation of God and man is further enhanced when Berdyaev talks of the divine-human personality of man. Moving man so close to God will certainly alarm a good many traditional Christians. Does not all of this closeness between God and man in the realm of the spirit contradict the view of man as the creature of God, of Jesus as the only God-man, and of God as being infinite, absolute, and all powerful?

God. The surprises will hardly end at this point for traditional Christians who decide to follow Berdyaev further. In his teaching about God he shows a definite connection with the German mystic, Jacob Böhme. The point of juncture is the concept of the *Urgrund*. For Böhme the *Urgrund* is an irrational principle, it is will. *Urgrund* is that primordial freedom which antecedes being, even precedes God himself. It represents the great cosmological mystery. Accordingly Böhme speaks about it only in the language of myth and symbol. Berdyaev's concept of God is deeply influenced by Böhme's idea of the *Urgrund*. God is not the "last" point of reference. He rather emerges out of that bottomless abyss which primordial freedom is. In it there is the mysterious urge of the nothing to become something. Out of the Godhead, deeply embedded in the meonic freedom, comes God, a God who no longer rules over everything and is not responsible for all happenings. He did not even create the world. To say that he did is to objectify and by it degrade the mystery of the spirit. It also diminishes the greatness of God. As creator and Lord he cannot but be responsible for all the evil and the terrible in the world.

All the theories of Divine Providence, the subtle explanations of evil as a lack of good, or the rest of the monisms which struggle so hard to preserve God's majesty and purity are in vain. God must be dissociated from the objective world. Objectification, as has been said before, is the "fall," is evil, and is that which must be overcome. God is not in the institutions of this world, however often they are pronounced "holy." He is not in disease, in terror, in any war, not even in the sense of a stern judge who uses these means to show his justice. All of this belongs to objectification, the great "fall," in which spirit loses itself in the world of external objects. God is neither subject to this process of objectification nor is he its originator. God should be thought of avoiding all images taken from society, man, and the cosmos. He must be seen as belonging to the realm of spirit alone—as spirit, love, and freedom.

God is not an absolute since this would make him self-sufficient. Far from being that, he needs the relation with man. He waits for man's answer to his call. He is not being as such, but spirit, which for man is at the same time his innermost core and a supreme mystery. Into this mystery of the spirit and God man can penetrate a certain distance. Rationality will help him for a part of his journey. The deepest penetration will result from a life led in the awareness that man is a dweller in the realm of spirit. It is in such an existence (Berdyaev's authentic existence) that the only possible communion with God is achieved, since God cannot be found in nature, which is objectification per se. God reveals himself to man in the true depth of man's personality and with the help of those moments which disrupt the seemingly smooth connection between man and the routine world (death, anxiety, and despair). The experience of God, for Berdyaev as for the other existentialists, is bound to the achievement of a full personality (authentic existence) and the awareness of estrangement (Berdyaev's "fall" or objectification) from the ground of one's being.

God, man, and the end. Christianity has always been keenly aware of the problems of eschatology, that is, the problems of death, immortality, judgment, the last day, and resurrection, but not radically enough to suit Berdyaev. First, there has been throughout Christian history a constant tendency to de-emphasize eschatology in favor of the attempt to Christianize the world, a hopeless endeavor in a world which for Berdyaev is a fallen one and not God's own. To build "the" Christian state, with Christian institutions involving Christians, is an illusion. Such a Christianity amounts to a new crucifixion of Christ. "There is nothing more horrifying and more gloomy than the objectification in history of that fire which Christ brought from heaven. Supreme failure has defeated all the great constructive efforts of history, and all designs which planned the social ordering of man."[39] Second, man has built up vengeful and cruel eschatologies, all of which have been modeled from the objectified world. The most outstanding example is the concept of hell. Those who adhere to it fail to see that such an eschatology of vengeance leaves God powerless in one spot, namely, in the place of damnation. For their own satisfaction, derived from seeing sinners suffer, they sacrifice the grandeur of God. Hell can only be in the phenomenal, the temporal, the objective world; otherwise it has no room in Christian thought because beyond the objective world lies the realm of the spirit and freedom where hell can find no place.

Thus, for an eschatological Christian neither the depreciation of eschatological awareness nor eschatologies modeled after the objectified world will do. Eschatology must remain the basis and the end of all. Berdyaev asserts that all thought leads to the problem of the end, an end which will not occur in the ordinary vitiated time (that connected with the fallen world) nor outside of time in some other world. It is not an event to be located in time as physics uses it, namely as a fourth dimension, nor in historical time. The end occurs in existential time. "It is only in existential time, which is to be measured by the degree of vigour and tension in the condition of the subject, that the way out towards eternity can be made clear. . . . That which we project into the sphere of the external, and call the end, is the existential experience of contact with the noumenal, and with the noumenal in its conflict with the phenomenal. The experience is not one of development from one stage to another, it is an experience of shock and catastrophe in personal and historical existence."[40] Here Berdyaev clearly shows that the end is as much a personal event as it is a beginning of a new era, or as he puts it, the new aeon.

The end means that objectification has been overcome. It signifies the great triumph over the recurrent and tragic "fall" that is the alienation and slavery of the spirit to the realm of necessity. The world of objects, so unfortunate for man, will be ended. There will be no more cooling of the creative fire.

Far from being destructive, this end is actually the source of all meaning. A world without a definite end would be a boring sequence of events which hardly matter, since none of them would really differ from another. On the other hand, death as the absolute end of man's life also would destroy real meaning. And so for Berdyaev the end remains the center radiating meaning in all directions. Quite unorthodox is his interpretation of this new aeon, ushered in by the end, as the third, the eschatological revelation. Before it went God's revelation first in nature and then in history. The third revelation is that in which God reveals himself fully and finally. It comes after a state of God-forsakenness characterized by the features so typical of our era.

It may be difficult to see at once the connection between this undoubtedly visionary and, to many, utopian view and existentialist thought. This bridge is the position which man, according to Berdyaev, takes in the great event of the end. The end is not because of a divine decree. The great decisions fall in each and every individual existence. Everybody's decision for or against freedom in his own life determines the course the future will take. The end is the common task of all men, rather than an event mankind passively waits for. Every creative work of man is a contribution to the final transformation of the world and the resurrection of every creature. In any authentic existence the end is always present as its focus. Personality is fulfillment here and now, but it also points beyond itself to the coming of the new aeon. Thus man is put back into a field of tension between the old and the new, the objective world and his participation in the realm of freedom, to live in a fallen way (given to objectivity) or to be authentic as God's co-worker toward the coming of the end. At every moment the challenge to decide is present. There is no "neutral" moment. Berdyaev demands with Kierkegaard either/or. Either living from the ground of one's being (freedom) or estrangement in a life given to the world of objectivity.

Ethics. With God not the creator of the world the problem of evil has been shifted. Evil is not just something which is less real than good, perhaps just a lack of good. Evil is real. It does not belong to the realm of spirit and freedom, but has its roots in the realm of objectivity. Evil is inseparably linked to the mystery of objectification. Ethics, as the guide for man to the absolutely good, must center around man's setting himself free from the fallen world. No ethical code will do, however. For man to subject himself to a code of ethics would mean to enter a new slavery. Only freedom can give the basis for a moral life. So everyone is on his own, must be on his own. Freedom and creativity cannot be caught and expressed in rules. "Be creative" is the core of Berdyaev's ethics. No other specific admonition can be given, since to be free means to be unique in a unique situation. No concrete rule is pliable enough to fit all situations. Not fitting most of them, it results in deadly slavery for the unique and free man.

Social philosophy. The dualism between spirit and objectification also forms the point of departure for Berdyaev's social philosophy. He acknowledges that man is a social being, that sociality is an aspect of the human life. Society has two aims: (a) co-operation in the common effort of men in the struggle for life which enables the human race to survive, and (b) community in the union of men who live authentically. Western man has been successfull in his efforts toward co-operation. Tragically so, since it is especially in this sphere that the pitfalls of society become obvious. Such a society participates in the process of objectification. At its very basis is the fall. While it is useful to man, it harbors tremendous dangers for him, above all the danger of slavery to objectivity. For Berdyaev all contemporary social institutions of man are examples of this slavery. On the same level are the natural theories of society. These are wrong both in suggesting a so-called natural order underlying the social phenomena and in promising to know the perfect social order. There can be no fulfillment in this sphere of objectivity. Even a Christian society is possible not as a perfect hierarchy of power but only as a free union of men in the spirit of brotherhood. This anarchic community of free men, free in the sense of "meonic," creative freedom, is Berdyaev's suggestion for the social life of man, an anarchism which differs from ordinary anarchism in every respect.

There is one strange inconsistency in Berdyaev's social philosophy which is probably the result of his personal experiences. It appears in his personalist socialism. Berdyaev, like Buber, sees the proper order of the economic life in a socialistic organization. To him it is that order alone which can guarantee personal autonomy. Personalist socialism differs from the now prevailing collective socialism in its aim. It tries to free man from the state rather than to subdue him to it. As to its exact form, we are left with the impression that it would have as its maximum organization a community of communities similar to that suggested by Buber, if it had even that much form. The inconsistency lies in the admittance of any supposed superiority of one form of organization over another, since on his own terms they can all be only parts of the objective world. Berdyaev wrote at this point most certainly out of his deep resentment against both the *ancien régime* of Russia under the Czars and the communist utopia. His only valid answer to the social problem could be his always implied spiritual anarchism.

IV. Existentialism Assessed

By now it should have become clear that existentialism is neither the fad nor the morbid philosophy some accuse it of being. The accusation of its being a fad or deteriorating into one is based on the spectacle which was made of it in Paris in the years following the Second World War. There existentialism shared the fate of any philosophy which reaches beyond the small circles of professional philosophers. While such a fate permits a philosophy to become influential with a larger number of those intellectually concerned, it also leaves it helplessly open to those who grasp one or another of its ideas and build around it a cheap sensationalism. A group of such, claiming to be existentialists, substituted beards, confused and incoherent writing, and turtleneck sweaters for substantial ideas. They never were and will never be existentialists. Existentialism is far too serious a philosophy to be discarded just because a few have misused it for their own purposes.

Nor is the accusation that existentialism is a morbid philosophy justified. Admittedly there is in existentialism an overemphasis on such human experiences as suffering, despair, anxiety and death. Compared with the attention these recieve, the emphasis on other human experiences like joy and love seems negligible, except for the works of the religious existentialists. But this is hardly enough reason for the label of morbidity. The experiences apparently overemphasized have in existentialist philosophy no mere negative importance. It has been shown how necessary and constructive they are for the forming of authentic existence. The overemphasis can also be understood as a reaction to that mode of thought which not only underestimates despair, anxiety, suffering and death, but makes a point of ignoring them.

Existentialism is an absolutely serious philosophy. It has become extremely influential in continental Europe and has been slowly gaining ground in the Anglo-Saxon world. What it has to say merits the attention of every thinking person. Whether in the end he agrees or disagrees with it, he will be left with the impression that the problems of man are being dealt with in a thoroughly sincere manner, one that is telling for our age.

A. The Existentialist Image of Man and His World

Existentialism is primarily, sometimes one is tempted to say exclusively, interested in man. When it establishes new paths to God or the world, however, it becomes evident that this preoccupation is not to be equated with a simple anthropocentrism. For the existentialist man is the obvious point of departure, and accordingly every venture in philosophy must begin with him. Man's existence is the central fact which the existentialist never tires of analyzing and observing. Far from being just one of the aspects of what it means to be human, to exist is, as Sartre would say, the most brutal and naked fact man faces, one which cannot be escaped. In the fact that man exists really and uniquely originates all his interest in the world. It drives him into all his endeavors of thought because he realizes that in the end his life is at stake.

1. THE "NO" TO THE SO-CALLED SCIENTIFIC IMAGE OF MAN

Existentialists have unfailingly protested against the images of man formed and cherished by their contemporaries. From Kierkegaard on they have defended the unique existing individual, his freedom and his responsibilities. Since their various criticisms are, by now, well known it should be instructive to contrast the existentialist image of man with another contemporary view of man which is especially popular on the American intellectual scene. I refer here to the image of man as it appears in behavioristic psychology and the social sciences based on it. Existentialists are diametrically opposed to it. Indeed the mere contention that the mystery of human life has essentially been solved seems to the existentialists to be a tragic error. No less objectionable, however, is the content of the image itself.

The image of man which behavioristic psychology suggests and which it transmits to the social sciences is based on the Darwinistic theory with its shaping and re-shaping of organisms and their tools of adjustment according to the demands of a changing environment, and Ivan Pavlov's experiments with dogs which led to the formulation of the concept of the "conditioned reflex." According to it a certain stimulus will through proper conditioning of the organism evoke a particular and desired response. Far from being accepted as merely a valid insight into one aspect of organic, including human, behavior, the whole idea of mechanical conditioning soon came to be considered the fundamental theory of learning. As far as behavioristic psychology is concerned, all further development in knowledge about man will be more and more detailed illustrations of these basic insights achieved by an ever-increasing refinement of the methods and tools of observation. Man is thus seen as an organism with specific and highly favorable abilities for his survival. Although these make man the crowning achievement of nature, they in no way lift him out of the realm of nature. Actually all the human capacities and creations are merely refined instruments of adjustment. Everything from art to religion, from philosophy to the most intricate scientific theory, is understood as a tool of survival under given conditions. Consequently the supreme aim of man's life, like that of any other organism, is the mere satisfaction of all his wants and drives, of which the physiological are the basic ones. All the ideals of man expressed in various customs, whether monogamy or the democratic form of life, are viewed as habits, which have proved to be successful means of need gratification and, thus, survival. Their value is purely temporary since it depends on the changing environment.

The existentialist image of man presents a clear "no" to all of this. Existentialists view human life as both the supreme venture and the supreme mystery. For them it constitutes a dramatic event. Over against the organism with a passively accepted superstructure of habits, which behaviorists call man, the existentialists put the idea of the free and responsible man. This free and responsible man strives to form himself in the totality of his life. He knows of the uniqueness of his existence and admits its overpowering importance. He also knows about the polarity between unauthentic and authentic existence as he becomes aware of it in a wealth of human experiences. How he grapples with these insights forms the true drama of human life. That by virtue of such an approach the study of man becomes again a good deal more difficult, that it gains new depths, and that no simple formula will any longer suffice, the existentialists do not regret. To them it seems only a fair price to pay for the regaining of the lost dimensions of man and the study of man, in short, for the return of the man of flesh and blood to replace his pale shadow.

2. THE ELEMENTS OF THE HUMAN DRAMA

Unauthentic existence. At the very core of each philosophy has always been the wish to bring fulfillment to the human longing to find the meaning of life. The existentialists have held that such a fulfillment can come not from the creation of thought systems but only in authentic existence. Consequently, unauthentic existence is the direct antipode of fulfillment. It represents deficiency and negativity. Those who live in it are characterized by their abandonment to the anonymity of the "one does, one says" (Heidegger), the "everyday" (Jaspers) or to passive and literalist religiosity (Tillich,

Buber, Marcel, and Berdyaev). Kierkegaard spoke of a life led on the purely aesthetic level. In every case there is the strange sight of man who although deeply involved in his world remains inwardly indifferent and detached. Curiously it is this very life of unauthentic existence which much of modern psychology and the social sciences regard as a life of normalcy. The purely functional or organizational man is the archetype of the unauthentically living man.

The sharp discrepancy between the existentialist and the so-called scientific view of man appears most clearly in their respective attitudes toward conformity as an ingredient of existence. The ideal of adjustment, as it is reiterated over and over in modern psychology and the social sciences, regards conformity as a positive attitude. As a matter of fact, the whole mechanistic theory of learning (conditioning), whereby man automatically acquires the needed habits, is built on the desirability of conforming. That the existentialist is of another opinion has already been shown in the introductory example of Ivan Ilyich. During his life Ivan Ilyich abandons all thought of the special position each man holds, tries to forget that he should realize himself and not merely conform, and chooses to be like all the others. But the break from thoughtless conformity is necessary for the birth of an authentic living personality. What the existentialists aim at is certainly not superficial nonconformity. None of them has ever asked man to walk on his hands just in order to be different. All of them have conceded the necessity of some degree of conformity in civilized life. On the other hand, they have also called on man to view this as a necessary evil, because personality-forming is a lonely affair which never should find its guiding patterns outside. What the existentialists attack is conformity as a fetish. And what else does he make it who declares that the average is the standard of normalcy? The existentialists have been keenly aware of the fact that, as Pascal suggested, there can be a conflict between the conformity required by the customs of society and the upholding of one's personal integrity. The view of a perfect harmony between these two elements of human life is a dangerous error.

The existentialists, furthermore, imply quite rightly that although thoughtless conformity has been with man all through the ages, modern man can least afford to make it an idol. On the contrary modern man will have to fight such a conformity harder than any of his predecessors did. First he lives in a society which has at its disposal altogether too powerful means of compulsion to enforce an unprecedented conformity. Second, those indifferent to a truly human existence possess an enormous influence on all of modern life. If no attempt is made to recall each man to the duty of being free and responsible, the result will be a society which is a strait jacket of conformity and mediocrity. In such a society those creative and concerned will be lost in a mass of complacent automatons. That it furthers unauthenticity with all of its dreaded consequences is the gravest accusation hurled by the existentialist against those who form and hold the image of man as a bundle of functions and habits.

Unauthentic existence is to be overcome. It is the mere being in the world, driven and not driving. In it man has not yet overcome his estrangement from what is truly human. To remain in this state is not worthy of a human being, since it is the denial of the great potentialities of man. The doors by which to leave this lowest level of human existence are wide open for those who want to see them. They are opened by certain fundamental experiences shared by all mankind, but unfortunately explained away not only by modern psychologists but also by many philosophers and religious thinkers. Always there has been an attempt to lessen the impact of these experiences by finding a niche for them in thought systems. The existentialists have been demanding that the full immediacy of such experiences as anxiety, risk, boredom, despair, death and nothingness be preserved. Only then can they provide the jolt necessary to project man out of his unauthentic existence.

In the discussion of these experiences existentialists have always faced a dilemma which has never been fully resolved. What do I mean when I say "my anxiety"? If it is understood as a specific example of a general category, anxiety, then a traditional analysis of the category man would follow in terms of universal categories. This exhausting of the fact of existence in analysis and definition existentialists have been trying to avoid. On the other hand if I speak only of my anxiety, if there are only individual existents without overarching general concepts, what importance does my experience have for other men? Existentialists have never given a statement explaining away this difficulty. They have usually tried to solve the problem by speaking of one individual's experiences as a challenge to his fellow man to realize his own condition, a challenge, so to speak, to strike out on one's own. Hence the preference of existentialists for indirect communication, which guides man to his own experiences and does not teach in paragraphs (Jaspers' "appeal"). The experiences of one person are thus not in any way coercive for others but still of value to them.

Fundamental experiences. The existentialist emphasis on experiences like anxiety, despair, forlornness has led to a good many misunderstandings and much ensuing criticism. The most serious criticism has been the accusation that existentialism is a "mood philosophy," which has built its case on capricious states of mind and, thus, is completely irrational and hardly worth serious study. To everyone familiar with the writings of existentialists this is a definite misunderstanding. The experiences referred to are never thought of by existentialists as caprices. They are dispositions in which the full dimensions of human life become visible. They prove to be guides below the surface of the human life. Nor are these personal dispositions mere emotions. There is a place for rationality in these experiences, although they cannot be fully grasped by reason alone. Far from being an excess of emotionalism, existentialism is a personalistic philosophy in the sense of always being concerned with the whole, the living person. It emphasizes experiences like anxiety, despair, and others because they are important parts of the life of each person. The label of "mood philosophy" is definitely erroneous.

The first experience to be discussed must be *contingency*. The realization of the fragility of human life is abundantly reflected in existentialist writings in the clear recognition of the importance of man's birth into a strange world and his death, finitude, and temporality. The fact and experience of contingency does not lead to the same conclusions with all existentialists. For Kierkegaard it clearly shows the deep rift between man, the finite being, and God, the absolute. Sartre takes it as a challenge to man to become man in his short sojourn in this absurd world. Jaspers, carefully avoiding both views, sees the experience of contingency as a cipher pointing to transcendence. But all existentialists consider contingency as that shock which enables man to become aware of his special position among beings.

Contingency includes what Heidegger calls the awareness of "being-thrown-into-this-world." Man finds himself here in the world although no one has asked him whether he wanted to be here or not. Around him is a puzzling, often terrifying world. Similarly life ends with an event beyond man's control, death. It is the great event of human life, certain as to its occurrence, uncertain as to its specific date. Death is not only a terminal but also a personal event. Not even the ingenious twentieth century has found a way to die by proxy. Nor does man die in general as is implied in the popular saying "everybody must die" or in some theories and philosophies in which death is dealt with in one of a thousand paragraphs. Against all of this stands death as a brutal fact of human destiny. Heidegger speaks of death as "*je meiner*" (intrinsically my own) and Kierkegaard refers to it as "I and my death."

Far from ending with a romanticizing of death, however,

the existentialists transform it into the great force which can lead to an ennobling of man's life. Indeed it is one of the paradoxes of existentialism that by giving finitude a central place it transforms death into an enhancement of life. None of the existentialists advocates the Buddhist idea of a joyful greeting of death as the supreme relief from suffering, an annihilation of life which one hopes and strives for all through life. Such an exultation over death is just as mistaken as the ignoring of death. Western thought offers a good many ideas which depreciate death. Whether death is viewed as a purely natural event, the harvest of what has grown from seed to full-fledged plant, or as an incidental termination of a meandering life, it is deprived of its full impact. It is denied its role of making for a human life which at every moment is filled with an intensity of experience derived from the awareness that every moment is precious because in it a decision is made as to each individual's authenticity. The finitude of man's existence is actually that quality without which he would senselessly vegetate—if in this case he could be called man at all. It is the central challenge for Kierkegaard's existential Christian as it is for Sartre's atheistic existentialist. All of Heidegger's philosophy would collapse if the experience of finitude were to be taken from its central place. Secular and religious existentialists alike have insisted on contingency as the crucial mark of man's life. It alone initiates man's wondering about the meaning of life, projects him out of superficial comfort, and is the major challenge to an authentic life. For the existentialists it is a measure of the superficiality of most modern theories of man that they de-emphasize human finitude, mostly by exhortations to live as pleasantly as possible, forgetting everything else, making man act as if he lived on the level of other organisms. The significant result of such a misguided attempt is a world marked by a vanishing awareness of what man can be at his best.

Closely linked to contingency is the disposition of anxiety.

This term is particularly apt to be misunderstood, all the more as it enjoys considerable usage today. But a whole world separates the existentialist disposition of anxiety from the popular psychological concept of the same name. According to behaviorist psychology, anxiety results from maladjustment. Man is unable to meet the problems of his situation since he has not yet mastered the techniques of adjustment made available by his society. The consequence of this is man's failure to gratify his needs to their fullest extent. In early historical times this probably meant a threat to the survival of the maladjusted individual. Today it may mean only a lack of success. But always this anxiety is viewed as resulting from no more than a deviation from the "normal," the adjusted life. Anxiety might be defined as the result of a lack of ability to conform. As far as the existentialist is concerned, such a conception of anxiety moves exclusively in the area of unauthentic existence. Its disturbing implication is the call for strict conformity to the habits of thought and action exhibited by man's society, since it is presumed that they constitute the most perfect way of adjustment. The existentialist disapproves such an analysis of human anxiety and proceeds to his own.

Anxiety has first of all clearly to be distinguished from fear, which is always associated with a particular object of fear. A person may be afraid of a dark room although he knows nobody threatens him in it. Such fears can be overcome by various means. Anxiety, however, does not have the same source as fear. Nor is it explainable as a vague fear of physical nonsurvival or as a product of experiences resulting from incomplete adjustment. For secular and religious existentialists alike, anxiety is linked to the emerging awareness of nothingness; whether it be Kierkegaard's still Christian idea of damnation, Heidegger's nothingness which brings dynamics into Being, or Sartre's purely destructive nothingness. The differences do not matter at this point. Always nothingness is experienced in the contingency of man's life and with it as the awesome certainty of the "not to be," an experience not to be forgotten because of its supposed unpleasantness but on the contrary to be put at the core of man's life. Nothingness taken in this sense becomes the great positive force in man's life through its challenge to live authentically. With it anxiety is no longer the feeling of being threatened in one's physiological survival but is transformed into one of the most important guides man has to what he is beyond his organic life. Consequently anxiety is the call to become oneself rather than the signal for an increased or improved conformity. Anxiety bares to man the state of non-being, which, viewed objectively, is only an interesting facet of all life. Anxiety results whenever nothingness through contingency has been understood by man in its immediate importance for each person.

Even more transparent as to the tensions it reveals and the forces which are at work to show man his way to authenticity is the existential disposition of despair. Here man is totally submerged in that whirlpool of freedom in which alone he can find his way to an authentic existence. He is lifted out of the security offered by his social and political institutions, by philosophical systems, by scientific world views, by his daily routine—in short out of any comforting feeling of being already "at home." In despair the certainty of any haven of safety turns out to be illusory. Existential despair is becoming aware of one's being alone in those matters which count most. Where a man's life is at stake no other man and no human institution can lift the burden of responsibility and decision from his shoulders. Nor does authentic existence, as the existentialist answer, obliterate this whirlpool of freedom. The very way by which authentic existence is arrived at prevents this. No smooth transition leads from existential despair to authentic existence. The bridge is not one which can comfortably be crossed. Ever since Kierkegaard, existentialists have spoken of the leap into authentic existence. The leap is executed in a typical situation of human decision; that is, the leap itself and what it leads to never loses the character of being a great risk. Despair allows man to experience the realm of freedom in which true choices are made.

Authentic existence. This sudden breakthrough of man from all that is given to him, that he had been integrated into, and that had covered his real potentiality into the openness of true freedom is the crucial point in all existentialist works. It means both the end of estrangement and man's becoming an authentic existence. It is well to remember at this point that what is referred to here is not one blessed moment of conversion but a style of life in which despair and authenticity are never far distant from each other. Of course, existentialists disagree on the interpretation of this authenticity. Heidegger, for whom estrangement is a life detached from Being as the ground of all beings, sees authenticity as a human life led in awareness of its "standing-out" of this Being and in finding a way "home" to it. Death is the great caller to such a life, because through it man faces the mystery of Being (and nothingness) in all earnestness. For Sartre authenticity is creation of meaning. Like Nietzsche he wants man to know himself to be alone and without support from God. To be authentic is to be creative in spite of the ultimate futility of creation. Jaspers calls man to an authenticity which is essentially a determination continuously to journey—the aim being variously called the encompassing, transcendence, and God. To affirm wholly, yet nevertheless to go beyond this position and to affirm again endlessly, never getting tired of the journey, never stopping this personal advancing toward the last horizon by "accepting" so-called last truth, or living a routine life, or denying any meaning to the world—all this means to live authentically.

Religious existentialists have interpreted the existentialist breakthrough into the openness of freedom as one which enables a true human experience of God. The I becomes really I by personally, that is unconditionally, relating itself to God in freedom. This is so in Kierkegaard, Tillich, Marcel, Buber, and Berdyaev. Their insistence on this, the existential God-man relation, is probably their most important contribution to a genuine religious renaissance of our time, one which has nothing to do with increase in church membership but which recalls into the center of religious life the personal encounter of man with God. If he wishes, modern man can again find a way to a vigorous religious life, a way which is blocked neither by creeds, describing God in detail, nor by scientific theories seemingly excluding God.

The importance of this part of existentialism, namely its call for an authentic existence, can hardly be overemphasized. It constitutes the great rebirth of genuine individualism in a time which has lost the ardent desire for it despite all outwardly expressed enthusiasm. Or as Kierkegaard saw it, "Being an individual man is a thing that has been abolished, and every speculative philosopher confuses himself with humanity at large, whereby he becomes something infinitely great—and at the same time nothing at all."[1] Existentialists of all shades have called attention to the fact that no professed love of mankind has meaning as long as the free and responsible person is at the same time destroyed. Existentialist authenticity, whatever its critics may say against it, restores this person in all his freedom and responsibility. Those who speak of the supposed nihilistic tendency in existentialism utterly misunderstand its aims.

3. A PESSIMISTIC IMAGE OF MAN?

Another serious problem is posed by those who, after a study of existentialism, call at least secular existentialist philosophies the pinnacle of pessimism. At first sight this seems not too far-fetched. One remembers such words as anxiety, despair, and death. Even a closer look at what various secular existentialists consider an authentic existence appears to support the label of pessimism. Heidegger's authentic man is aware of his ultimate death and lives accordingly. No consolation in the traditional sense is offered. Sartre's man spends himself and in death meets an end which has challenged him to be man but still means his total annihilation. Jaspers, the most outspoken of them all at this point, directly and openly admits that even authentic existence ends in failure. Truly a tragic sense of life prevails in existentialist philosophy. But is it pessimism?

Many of the charges of pessimism come from people who miss in it a clearly spelled out message of salvation, whether in the form of a promised heaven beyond or a Golden Age here on earth. Where is any such hope for the existentialist? True, the existentialists are hesitant to offer any clear message of salvation in the traditional sense. The religious existentialists imply ultimate communion of man with God. But they, too, are much more concerned with the quality of the life led on earth and man's relation with God in it than with speculations about the exact details of an afterlife. The secular existentialists are even more restrained. Sartre, the atheist, denies any implication of a "beyond." Heidegger is silent on this topic though he leaves the door ajar, admittedly not too far. Jaspers speaks of the encompassing as the ultimate aim, again in indirect terms. Those who want a clear message of salvation will understandably not be satisfied with such little promise. Still there is more hope in existentialist philosophy for man than in any naturalistic philosophy. Man in all versions of existentialist philosophy, except Sartre's, is rooted "somewhere," however unspecific this may be, as it is in Heidegger and Jaspers. A meaningful life can come from this rooting. But where, despite all promises of a Golden Age, is there any reason for optimism in a naturalistic philosophy of man? Can it be found in viewing man as an organism concerned with his mere physiological survival, even taking into account his greatest accomplishments? Eventually such a man dies in absolute futility.

It is indeed strange that the so-called scientific image of man should be so widely viewed as optimistic. This comes, of course, from the fascination with mankind and its improvement which nearly all naturalistic philosophies exhibit. In this case one forgets that the individual life loses all true importance. A larger and more prosperous mankind compensates for the absolutely disregarded and unfulfilled quest for a meaning to the individual person's life. Such a life is actually no more elaborate than that of any organism. Birth, adjustment to conditions, and death are its whole content. Is this not the real pinnacle of pessimism? Can an ever so glorious destiny for mankind really compensate for the lack of meaning of the individual life? The existentialist insists that the meaning of life must be more than a mere reflection of "greater destinies." It must carry personal character in all of its aspects, in the way man is related to whatever gives meaning, in his responsibility for this relation, and in the freedom in which the relation is established.

All that is left of the criticism of existentialism as a supposedly pessimistic philosophy is then the lack of a promise and an exact topography of salvation. To this the existentialist answers that this lack of rational certitude is not indicative of a deficiency in existentialist philosophy, but rather that any philosophy which deals with man as a whole and living person will soon find this lack of certainty expressive of man's special position in the universe, being neither an animal nor God. Being more than what he is born as or made into by his environment he must constantly strive to become truly man. Losing and gaining himself alternately he shows the strange and fascinating restlessness of the "going from" and the "going to." The existentialist image of man tries to reflect this without at the same time freezing all of human life into a system of concepts. It wants to guide just enough to let man see his way but not to be coercive as to the direction he takes. The price such a philosophy must pay will always be the lack of absolute certainty in what it suggests, including the lack of a glittering promise of salvation.

4. MAN AND HIS WORLD

One of the more stringent criticisms of existentialism concerns its apparent unwillingness to create a philosophy of nature, some of its critics even say its inability to do so. Interestingly, there is a parallel in this respect to another period of Western thought. Before the penetration of the main works of Aristotle into Western thought, the medieval mind was shaped by the Augustinian view of the world. It centered exclusively on God and man. Thus St. Bernard of Clairvaux of the twelfth century is said to have traveled across the most beautiful landscapes without even noticing them. His concern with his soul and God left no room for occupation with matters seemingly so unrelated to it. Something similar, without the exact Augustinian implications of the "fallen" nature of the world, happens to the existentialist. Man and his life and its rooting in something beyond itself preoccupies most of the existentialists. This fascination is so strong as to exclude other concerns.

Another formidable obstacle to an existentialist philosophy of nature has certainly been the influence of Husserl's phenomenology, especially on Heidegger and Sartre. If man "brackets," that is, temporarily stores away, the question of what the world "outside" is, if he concerns himself only with the relations of the I with the world (that, and how, I see something, smell something, love something), if the "bracketed" world becomes through his particular experiences his own, within him—then he can hardly proceed to a philosophy of nature in the traditional sense. The world has become a part of the self. The modern scientist has chosen the other way. For him the world stays "outside." He always is vis-à-vis to it. It does not form him, he supposedly only observes and describes it. The world of the scientist is neutral, since it remains totally "outside" of his personality. The world of the existentialist is charged with quality, since it is fused with man's personality and totally "inside."

Characteristic of all of this is Heidegger's "being-thrown-in-the-world" by virtue of which everything is no longer *vorhanden* (just there) but *zuhanden* (there for me). Other persons assume the quality of *Mitsein* (to be with). Heidegger here brings to light the existentialist insistence on the relational man. His personality is intimately related to the world and to others. The existentialist does not speak of "I and" everything else but of "I in" and "I with" it. The world is not just a stage; as each man's situation is a part of man's self. St. Bernard ignored the "fallen world," the existentialist denies only the neutral world, that is the world of the scientist which does not speak to man but waits to be handled by him. The world as a part of his personality the existentialist not only acknowledges but embraces wholeheartedly. Any existentialist, secular or religious, differs, thus, from a mystic who excludes the world in favor of his most intimate concern with God. The situation which is with me as a part of my life, into which I am interwoven, must be affirmed as such. Nietzsche's *amor fati* resembles this standing of man in and with his situation. How I am interwoven into a world not of my choosing, how I fight in it for my integrity, how in loneliness I master my "being-thrown-into-the-world"—all this is the great drama of an authentic existence.

In the age-old controversy over what is "real" in the world, the existentialist stands at equal distances from the idealist and the materialist. The idealist tries to dissolve the tension between the I and the world by explaining the world as a mere projection of the mind. The materialist, on the other hand, submerges the I into the vast sea of matter. Indeed much of the so-called scientific image of man is based on the latter view, which consequently espouses unmitigated determinism of one sort or the other. This denial of all freedom leads to the paradox of the scientist observing, describing, and theorizing on a world in a supposedly objective way, while all along the world rules and drives him. The existentialist on the other hand never denies the reality of either the I or the world, and carefully preserves the tension between the two. The world is mine but still remains strange. That it is here, I experience as a brutal fact (Sartre). But no trick can give man the knowledge of what it is and, thus, make his world a comfortable place to live. Neither a denial of the reality of the world (idealist position) nor the denial of the uniqueness of man (materialist position), nor a set of benevolent laws of nature nor Divine Providence can eliminate the fundamental fact of the human condition, that no miraculous harmony exists in the world and that to resolve the enormous tension between man and his world is beyond human power. What becomes audible in this tension is the echo of man's questions reflected from "somewhere," and human life at its best is this sounding of the depths. The tension also is a challenge to proceed with this sounding all life long. The existentialist considers it his merit to have rediscovered this tension in all its severity. He did not, however, create it in his philosophy, as some critics would have us believe. Both the personal character of man's world and his being a stranger in it everyone can discover for himself in his own life.

B. Existentialists on Truth and God

Whatever is considered man's central concern, whether it be immortality of some sort or just the plain giving meaning to one's life, will always be intimately connected with the problem of truth. In his longing for truth man throughout the centuries has given expression to the desire for certitude. Because at the core of all this concern with truth stands the desired moment in which man can say: "Now I know. The world is clear to me and so is my position in it." All the ingenuity of man has been devoted to arriving at this moment of fulfillment.

Western thought has developed a number of theories as to which is the best way to get to the longed-for destination. In the process much of Western thought has, according to the existentialists, somewhere lost sight of the crucial fact that truth is not sought for truth's sake but as the answer to the most fervently asked personal question "who am I"? The nineteenth century was filled with experiments to find truth in a highly impersonal sense, as a system of supposedly generally valid statements about man and his world. When Kierkegaard and Nietzsche revolted against such an idea of objective truth they met with derision or were ignored. But existentialism has held fast to what can be considered one of its crucial assertions, namely that truth has a personal character. Far from being mere correspondence of thought with objective facts or coherence of a set of judgments, truth, according to the existentialists, is a judgment on the way one lives. This close connection between individual existence and truth has led to the grave, even crucial, criticism of existentialism that its truth is not truth at all but purely subjective philosophizing, the validity of which goes no further than the individual's own private world; in short, that existentialism has no contribution to make to the age-old human quest for certitude. While the problems brought about by the existentialist interpretation of truth should not be altogether denied it will, however, be maintained here that the contribution of existentialism to the endeavor of man to find truth is not only a valid but also a considerable one.

1. TRUTH AS INDIVIDUAL CONCERN

All existentialists have insisted that truth is closely tied to the individual human life. At first this seems to contradict the commonly held conception of truth as being so general in nature that it can be accepted by everybody as easily as the air we breathe. From such a standpoint an intimate connection between individual life and truth must of necessity appear to be a grave mistake. But while the existentialists have never abandoned their emphasis on truth as an individual concern, there has always been within existentialism an awareness of that aspect of truth which is usually called its generality. Existentialists have never disregarded the danger of leading all talk of truth *ad absurdum* by sponsoring a subjectivism which would substitute individual fancies for a genuine content of truth. The subjectivity of existentialist truth is in no sense the undisciplined and irresponsible building of dream worlds. This assertion can be shown to be correct by a look at what existentialists since Kierkegaard have said in this regard.

In Kierkegaard's work, as we have seen, the "what-truth-is" takes second place to "how-truth-is." What one can know objectively and distinterestedly, namely the relation and the gap between the infinite absolute and the finite man, is not much. But this lack of content is deceptive. To know, or better to experience it, means to feel challenged. Consequently there develops in man a process of truth. Gradually his whole life can become truthful in the sense of being filled with truth, although the truth to be grasped, if expressed in statements, is meager. The individual, inward, aspect of truth is held over against truth as the purely general truth. That two parts of hydrogen and one part of oxygen form water is such a general truth. It can be proved, is highly probable and for particular purposes extremely useful. Existentialists have never called for the abandonment of man's endeavor to build such a body of objective knowledge. Modern Western man has certainly benefited greatly from it. Existentialists have, however, never failed to point out that there are definite limits to any attempt to explain all that human life means through the approach of objective truth. Kierkegaard points to the fact that where it matters most man cannot expect truth to become visible without a passionate concern. It is the tragic error of those who strive solely after objective knowledge that at the bottom of their search there is a little appetite or curiosity to know but no sense of deep involvement.

Following Kierkegaard, Nietzsche and Sartre abolished even the last bit of positive content in the area of truth. The world as such is meaningless—this is all man can know. Beyond it every part of knowledge is knowledge of what I or other men have done. In these acts alone truth is contained. I and others set it. The most perfect knowledge of what has happened at this or that point can never be true. For Nietzsche and Sartre truth lies in the act of setting meaning. Here Kierkegaard has found successors much more radical than himself. Truth is purely individual, inward and activistic, although Sartre speaks of choices made for all mankind. But existentialism has had thinkers who have tried to combine the what and the how aspects of truth more harmoniously. Some of the twentieth century's existentialists have even openly aimed at building an ontology. Heidegger, for example, has all along been claiming that he aims at a philosophy of Being. If this is so, a good many statements which one can "know" may come forward. Up to now, his philosophy has centered around man as he is grounded in Being. What one can know in Heidegger's work is just as limited as it is in Kierkegaard's. How the truth is affirmed is still the predominant note, and it is this fact which gives us the right to speak of Heidegger as an existentialist. Jaspers, too, tries carefully to balance in his philosophy the universally valid encompassing a common bond with *Existenz* as the individual assertion of the truth in which man stands. The cipher, the message of transcendence, is at the same time a piece of general knowledge and a challenge to the individual to go beyond it.

Despite these attempts to do justice to truth as possessing generality, it still is true that in existentialism that aspect of truth which is most intimately connected with individual life is heavily emphasized. The existentialists from Kierkegaard on have always insisted that truth lies not in an all-comprehensive system of thought which is put into print and read by curious but unconcerned readers. Truth, as is implied if one speaks of truth as an individual concern, must be lived in order to become truth.

2. TRUTH AS TRUTH LIVED

The prevalent attitude in the contemporary endeavor to get closer to truth, symbolized by the sciences, is that of a spectator. He looks at everything as an object outside himself even when he observes himself. He observes, registers, counts, and theorizes. But nothing striven and searched for and eventually found really penetrates into the depth of his personality. The main criticism existentialists level against the development of Western thought, especially since Descartes, is that even when man doubts he merely acts as if he doubted. The seeker of truth himself stands outside his search and, as Marcel puts it, wants to possess truth—a truth which is the truth of the observer and manipulator. Against this view existentialists put their conception of truth which deeply and personally involves the one who searches for it. Consequently, beginning with Kierkegaard, one senses the difficulties each existentialist has had in communicating and teaching his truth. They have all finally chosen to "appeal" instead of teaching in statements. Such an "appeal" that is to guide man until his own process of truth is "ignited" has no room in systematic truth. Systems are monuments of non-existential truth and with it the main targets of existentialist criticism. The criticism is directed against every kind of supposedly all-inclusive systems, metaphysical, scientific or others. They all start from one or more fundamental propositions. The world is then made to appear in the light of the assumption made, all neatly formulated. Man, the eternal puzzle to himself, for example, may be found explained in part two, paragraph three, lines five to ten of such a system. All of this is fascinating since man need do no more than read one systematic work and suddenly he knows how to explain everything, including his own life. After that he can relax, the world is no longer a problem.

The existentialists have turned out to be spoilsports. Does all this brilliant coherence show more than that one knows the rules of deducing and inducing? Furthermore, is the world in its fullness, is man as he lives, really contained in these systems? Can the world as it presents itself to man ever be a system? Have not the system builders, in order to fit man into their systems, first to slay the man of flesh and blood? Does the system builder not all too often first define man as he wants to see him, and then interpret actually existing man according to his own definition? These are only theoretical dangerous consequences of system builders. For each and every man there are other, more serious repercussions. The I which finds itself defined as part of a vast world system is left only the task of filling its place in it. The concrete I is merely one of the numerous manifestations of a special category of beings. Uniqueness and the sense of the immediacy of personal experience have no room in the generality of the system. The importance which each person attaches to his life appears ridiculous if viewed from the vantage point of the system. But as Kierkegaard puts it: "Abstract thought is disinterested, but for an existing individual existence is the highest interest."[2]

Another danger shows in the temptation to accept a certain system of truth in thought only. In the realm of everyday life this accepted system has then no consequences. The truth man holds about himself and the world, he holds like all his other possessions. It is comparable to the first aid box in a car. It is a comfort to know that it is carried along on trips for use in emergencies. At this point the quality of systems appears which meets one of the sharpest criticisms of the existentialists. True, the thinker who creates the system is at least honest in his intentions. He experiences the existential concern which in the end leads him to create his system. Systems with their supposed all-explaining capacity have, however, the fatal quality of fascinating those who do not want to grapple with the challenges of their own existence. For them, the inert and uninspired ones, the system, metaphysical or scientific, comes to be the ready delivered answer and the perfect tranquilizer. It soothes since it explains everything, whether earthquakes or the fragrance of the lily of the valley. Disturbing disharmonies and the chaos ever present in the world appear in such systems either as benevolent forces after all or as minor footnotes to an otherwise well-ordered scheme. For human life, too, all the answers are contained in the system. In most systems there is, for example, no room for real human failures. The general triumphs completely over the "single one," that is over the authentic and responsible individual. Instead of enhancing the existence of the individual person, the system integrates it, swallows it up and gives it the doubtful comfort of the "knowing" and "being carried on" by forces more powerful than himself.

In contrast to abstract, systematic truth, existential truth always remains incomplete. Lessing once put what existentialists have considered to be the supreme characteristic of the human quest for truth in a wish: "If God held all truth hidden in his right hand, and in his left hand the persistent striving for truth, and while warning me against eternal error, should say: 'Choose!' I should humbly bow before his left hand, and say: 'Father, give thy gift; the pure truth is for thee alone.' "[3] Still, most existentialists would admit that man in his centuries-old search has created islands of knowledge. But useful and beautiful as they may be, they tend to show man even more clearly the vastness of the mystery of his own existence. The word mystery should by no means be given a false connotation. The existentialists, with the exception of Sartre, all imply that the world has meaning and order. Still, an existential system of truth cannot be formed, because as Kierkegaard sees it, "an existential system cannot be formulated. Does this mean that no such system exists? By no means; nor is this implied in our assertion. Reality itself is a system—for God; but it cannot be a system for any existing spirit."[4]

Actual existence by its very nature is never final, in the sense of being complete. Man is a system, but can never know this system in its entirety. How can man then at any time act as if he knew everything when to be able to know everything he himself would have to be "pure thought"? Even if everything else had stopped existing and thus were offering itself as an object for speculation and theorizing, the thinker himself would still exist. Existence is not at an end. However, "existence must be revoked in the eternal before the system can round itself out; there must be no existing remainder, not even such a little minikin as the existing *Herr Professor* who writes the system."[5] Accordingly the word "mystery" implies that the hope of generations to find the final truth must prove vain by virtue of the origin of thought in and its integration into the actual existence of the thinker. As he logically is never final as long as he lives, truth as a complete system of reality in which the thinker views himself as just one little part of it is impossible. His own actual existence betrays such an endeavor. "An actual emphasis on existence must be expressed in an essential form; in view of the elusiveness of existence, such a form will have to be an indirect form, namely the absence of a system."[6]

Heidegger and Jaspers have both proved in their works that such an absence of a system (in the pretentious sense of being final and all inclusive) need not prevent a thorough, exciting, and fruitful exploration of man. Even the religious existentialists have demonstrated that, although each of them stands within a definite religious tradition, the religious endeavor of man can be a vigorous and penetrating venture without metaphysical systems or the strict adherence to creeds and dogmas. While an existential system is impossible, existential truth is possible. It will, however, be tied to the existing individual and inculcate freedom, risk, anxiety, despair, and the incompleteness of existence itself. There will never be much in it which can be memorized or be disinterestedly observed, because existential truth revolves around the fundamental condition with its experiences of estrangement and authentic existence. It is possible to read what the existentialists have to say on each of these two points and still not possess truth as objective truth can be possessed. To existential truth belongs the process of appropriation by the individual; that is, standing in this truth, losing it, and finding it again. Existential truth is highly personal and must be searched for and found anew in every human life. "For the notion that from now on until the end of the world nothing could be said except what proposed a further improvement in an almost completed system, is merely a systematic consequence for systematics."[7]

To some this may all seem to be an utterly theoretical discussion. Does it really matter whether truth is subjective or objective? For them two practical implications of a decision on this question may be pointed out. Systems of objective truth have an intrinsically coercive tendency. In them an aspect of man's life is grasped, made the fundament of the system, and then declared to be the ultimate explanation of man and his world. Changes are limited to improvements of the system. After this single act of creation, all systems tend to begin a defensive action against other views. In the course of it the system claims both a monopoly of the "right" method and the "right" insights. Compromises, although eventually accomplished, are first ruled out. A case in point in the intellectual field is the systems of knowledge in the social sciences. The methods of the natural sciences, originally used only experimentally, have now become the only ones tolerated. Findings not documented by measurements, quantifications, and statistics are by virtue of this lack alone called unscientific, that is, worthless. Theories based on findings under the use of the "right" method and the "right" image of man are defended no longer as tentative theories but as systems of faith.

While this instance may concern only the academic world, one need only look into world history to see what happens whenever "objective" systems of truth gain the actual means of compulsion. The burning at the stake of those disagreeing with the official system has been no monopoly of any one period of history. This is only an extreme manifestation of the inability of adherents of closed systems of objective truth really to communicate with anybody who does not share their beliefs. Against this stands the openness of existential truth. Jaspers, who is clearest on this point, shows how much tolerance there is in existentialism. Those who do not possess absolute objective truth can never find justification for coercion. To coerce would destroy the other person's ability to find authenticity for himself. Jaspers speaks of the "loving struggle" which permits each existential truth affirmed to meet another existential truth affirmed in the spirit of co-operation and tolerance. Agreement will not be necessarily aimed at but may appear in what Marcel calls the identity of personal testimonies.

Another implication—briefly mentioned before—is less threatening only at first sight. Systematic bodies of objective truth foster human inertia by persuading the many that truth is confined to an acceptance of supposedly correct propositions about objects. To accept is the highway to truth. Who would hesitate to make a system his own which claims so much for itself, especially since the realm of thought in which this objective truth resides can be neatly separated from the realm of man's actual existence? The non-obligating character of objective truth is another danger very apparent in practice. It fails to destroy the wall of indifference which prevents altogether too many from leading a truly human life. Against it the existentialists hold that to know is not enough. Man must be grasped by truth.

3. EXISTENTIALISM: THE TRIUMPH OF IRRATIONALISM?

The idea that existentialism is the triumph of irrationalism has, oddly enough, been expressed by both the most ardent critics and admirers of existentialism. The former have said it to discredit this whole current of thought, the latter in the spirit of those who sense the promising dawn of a new era. Both claims are doubtful. As for the critics: if by irrationalism is meant the prevalence of instincts, moods, or intuition over reason, the classification of existentialism as one of its schools is misplaced. Although it is hard to make a general statement on this point, since the existentialists differ from each other as far as details are concerned, one can, however, say that they do not depreciate reason in favor of another single human faculty. Reason, on the contrary, is integrated into the totality of the human person. It is only logical that in the course of this integration the claim of reason to be the supreme tool of human world orientation is destroyed. But no new predominance of another human faculty is proclaimed. The key word existence itself shows how concerned existentialism is with the totality of the human person. Man does not exist solely or even primarily as reason or mood or instinct. Man is all of these in a complicated unity.

Some will point to Kierkegaard to prove that he at least was an irrationalist par excellence. It is true that reason is helpless before the great paradox of human life, that man longs as a finite being for communication with the infinite, the absolute. But it is reason itself which guides man to the awareness of the paradox. Reason delivers man to faith, which is personal and rational. The Kierkegaardian existence shelters a dialectic between reason and un-reason. To say this is, however, the same as saying that existence can neither be thought of nor lived under the exclusion of reason.

When Heidegger speaks at times of reason as the obstacle to right thinking, he, too, calls for a re-evaluation of reason rather than the discarding of it. How *Dasein* (or human existence) realizes being rooted in Being is again a question only to be answered by the total person. Man who hopes that his reason alone will suffice while the rest of his personality is left inactivated (non-involved) will fail. Reason or thought are not the bridge between the two distant shores of man and his world, but are faculties closely integrated into the whole man and into that in which he stands, Being. Thus neither reason alone nor the total lack of it will do.

Jaspers is even more specific as to the role assigned to reason. It makes its most remarkable contribution in the sciences and in philosophy when it guides man to the borderline of the objectively knowable. For man to begin his exploration without using what man by virtue of his reason has created in these two fields means to deliver himself to uncontrolled superstition. Jaspers makes a special contribution to the question of the role of reason when he distinguishes between its two roles —doubting and explaining. Reason as the explainer (*Verstand*) grasps the world through and in its elaborate analyses and definite statements. But the readiness of reason to doubt what it itself has found *(Vernunft)* connects reason intimately with the existentialist endeavor. While reason in the first interpretation seems and actually is opposed to the openness of truth, reason as the doubter is a necessary part of existence itself. Jaspers strongly emphasizes this connection.

As far as the supreme aim of all truth-seeking is concerned, namely to find the absolute point of certainty viewed from which the world would yield the answers to all its problems, all attempts have failed so far. At the beginning of every system stand assertions which no longer can be proved and which have to be accepted at face value. There has been no exception to this. Even the contemporary logical positivists have experienced this stubborn obstacle to a finally assured, universally valid truth. They have never been able to find those basic statements which directly reflect the world as it is (protocol sentences) without an intermediary interpretation by man. As a matter of fact the whole school of thought was split asunder in the controversy over where this last point of certainty lies. Are not all thinkers irrationalists of sorts, if reason proves to have a definite limit? And is that irrationalism which starts its inquiry with man as he lives and exists not the most preferable choice?

To say, therefore, that existentialism is irrationalism is a rather glib statement. Existentialism just does not fit into such a black and white picture. While existentialism denies the validity of the modern overemphasis on reason as the all-powerful and infallible explainer of the world, it has never called for the abandonment of it. More than at any other point the personalism of existentialism shows in this discussion of truth. In the true person (authentic existence), all faculties of man form a whole. In the course of their interplay one may temporarily outweigh the other. But it is the task of man to restore the integrated entity his personality ideally is by emphasizing and de-emphasizing wherever needed.

4. THE "LIVING" GOD

Those engaged in forming the modern image of man and his world have very little use for long discussions about the question of God. As a so-called "supernatural" phenomenon God falls by definition outside of that framework within which most psychologists and social scientists prefer to stay. God cannot be seen or heard like man, nor can one experiment with him nor quantify him. Thus, it is reasoned, he may be a useful imaginary person, but he cannot be said to exist in a meaningful way. In the universe of the behaviorist, God indeed has no meaningful place. What could and should his function be if everything were mechanistic? Consequently he is related to the realm of imaginary figures who, like Santa Claus in our infancy, excite, give hope and perhaps some security, but inevitably turn out to be fictitious. Mankind today has better tools of adjustment than such "supernatural" forces.

Even the atheists among the existentialists find a good deal to criticize in such a view. Nietzsche, the great revolutionary of the nineteenth century, called out "God is dead." But he was far from thinking this a joyous discovery. He wanted to point out that for most people of his period, scientists and indifferents alike, God was no longer a living reality. The consequences he foresaw were, however, radically different from those who displayed a glib confidence in the future glory of mankind, liberated from such "outdated" notions as God. Nietzsche suggested that what actually confronted man was the cruel choice between nihilism and a re-creation of man. Sartre, the atheistic existentialist, too, is far removed from the superficiality of other forms of atheism. For him the nonexistence of God is the most disquieting fact of human life. Man can only overcome its extremely harsh consequences by titanic efforts. Every man will have to make them. Neither mankind nor some set of benevolent natural laws can function as substitutes for God or for the necessary individual efforts.

Thus, even those atheistic thinkers who are in one way or other connected with existentialism point in their manner to the seriousness of the "God-forsakenness" of modern Western man. They refuse to share in the ease with which many modern thinkers do away with the question of God. They also reject the idea of letting individual man find a new and seemingly satisfactory shelter in the anonymity of mass society with its inquiry-dulling routine. According to Nietzsche and Sartre, those who do not have room for God in their thought and want to submerge the individual under various pretexts in the doubtful comfort of a life of conformity practice outright deceit. The real choice is nihilism or the rebirth of man. Such an assertion gives the announcement "God is dead" an entirely different tonal quality.

Thus, even the atheists among the existentialists display the seriousness which characterizes all existentialist discussion of God. This is not surprising, since they all determinedly deal with the whole and the living person. Of course, a man who finds fulfillment in his routine life as a functional part of his society and accepts a ready-made theory which justifies such a life does not need God. He closes himself against a relation to God—even if he nominally belongs to a church, because even in the routine of a church life God can be dead. Aside from Sartre all other existentialists have, on the other hand, in their attempts to point out the ways to overcome the estrangement of man, discovered the characteristic openness of the human personality toward the "beyond himself." In this way Kierkegaard finds God the infinite and absolute. Heidegger speaks of Being "out of which man stands" and toward which in authentic existence he is oriented. He refuses, however, to speak of God directly since, according to him, to do so would lead into pure speculation. "My philosophy is a waiting for God," he once stated. Jaspers demands of all genuine philosophy a clear commitment on the question of God. In his own philosophy he tries to clear a way for a faith without coercive assertions. The religious existentialists would, of course, be the least likely to underrate the problem of God and man's way to God.

The unanimity of the existentialists on the importance of the question of God disintegrates, however, when they give their respective interpretations. At one end of existentialism stands Kierkegaard, whose God, infinite and absolute, is the Christian God. He does not ask whether such a God exists. How to live a life in relation to that infinite and absolute God of Christian tradition alone forms the core of faith. If there is a Christian existentialism which is close to traditional Christian teaching it is the existentialism of Kierkegaard. Among modern existentialists Gabriel Marcel and Paul Tillich come closest to him. At the opposite end of the line stand the second of the revolutionaries of thought of the nineteenth century, Nietzsche, and the well-known atheist Sartre. Their denial of God is complete and outright. They put forth no cheap solution. The absence of God leaves a universe without pre-set meaning. Man, the new creator and master, sets it. Both philosophers have a nearly tragic sense for the unbelievable burden which such a responsibility place upon man. That atheistic humanism which is equipped with all kinds of safety valves preventing the pressure on individual man from rising too high (automatic progress, the goodness of man, refined social engineering, or benevolent natural laws) has accordingly found a greater number of followers. Nietzsche and Sartre, rightfully understood, are extremely unpleasant challengers. Their demands are as absolute as those of Kierkegaard without his point of ultimate hope.

Heidegger and Jaspers find their places between these two extremes. Heidegger's work contains a curious twofold implication for the religious question. At one time his analysis seems to be a soliloquy between man and Being. Man's whole existence acquires religious rigor, although nothing is said about God. On the other hand Being, this home of everything, offers room enough for a possible inclusion of God. Heidegger himself has never made it, partially perhaps because his final interpretation of Being has still not been given, partially to avoid the traditional error of too facile a treatment of God. Still, much of modern Protestant thought relies heavily on his work (Tillich, Bultmann). Jaspers paradoxically is at the same time more outspoken and even less definitive on the subject of God. He speaks of God quite readily but also declines to accept the validity of any particular religious tradition. God is found in the constant and purely individual search for one's relation to the horizon of transcendence from which all the messages (ciphers) are broadcast. Every man makes the decision whether these become challenges for him to become *Existenz* or are understood (better really, ignored) by interpreting them according to some pre-set schemes. Obviously Jaspers shares with other existentialists their distaste for creeds and dogmas. While he acknowledges the experiences of religious prophets as genuine, he still insists on the necessity for everyone to have his own experience of God. Each man must build his own street to God, avoiding the paved but deceptive highways offered by religious traditions. Furthermore, Jaspers denies any possibility of reaching God once and forever. The religious endeavor is part of the journey which for each authentically living man lasts as long as he exists. Religious certitude is, therefore, no possession man can gain once and for all.

It is this denial of a systematic metaphysics, of literally asserted and accepted creeds and dogmas as coercive truth, of the undoubted beneficence of religious organizations, and of prophetic religions which makes one wonder how existentialist philosophy could possibly have penetrated religious traditions. Actually the influence has been rather strong, although it must be admitted that neither Tillich nor Marcel nor Buber nor Berdyaev have become the idols of the masses. The last three have even been lonely figures in their respective traditions. Tillich's influence, by virtue of his teaching position and the enormous latitude inherent in Protestantism, has been considerably stronger. All of these thinkers have, however, shown that the existentialist image of man has something to say to every religious tradition. It has put back into the religious endeavor the awareness of the importance of true freedom, personal concern, risk, doubt, anxiety, and temporary despair. More significantly, the religious existentialists have made it impossible to think of religion as an operation in thought only. In the spirit of Kierkegaard all of them point to the personal character of man's relation with God.

Aside from the importance of these thinkers in the religious debate of the twentieth century, they have made a distinctive and decisive contribution to the modern scene by reviving the discussion of God within the confines of philosophy. After a period of an all too facile discarding of it, it should be possible from now on to speak out about God without being considered out of date, and without having to choose between the Scylla of a pseudo-scientific atheistic humanism and the Charybdis of a "proved" God or one pictured in dogmas and creeds. The existentialists have again opened to everyone the door to the religious realm in the spirit of a personal exploration. Those who prefer sophisticated theoretical discussions of God or those who are looking only for a consoling certitude will have no use for the existentialist position on God and his relation to man. Others, however, will find its possibilities intriguing.

C. Existentialist Ethics and Social Philosophy

1. THE PROBLEM OF RIGHT AND WRONG

A discussion of existentialism and ethics is apt to bring forth few ideas apart from those already mentioned. Existentialism is constantly concerned with the total person. Consequently ethical questions are touched upon all the time, since the very ideal set up for man by existentialists, authentic existence, gives every action of man immediately a positive or negative quality. Authenticity is the ultimate yardstick for calling a life, and with that all human actions, valuable or worthless. Unauthenticity, to lose oneself, is supreme evil. Although not at all representative of all of existentialism, Nietzsche shows most clearly the implications of such a position. Having abandoned an essential structure of the world and man, Nietzsche calls for a dynamic ethics. Values, as the products of bygone acts of creation, are of very little help in a situation which is strictly each man's own and thus unique. Nicely tabulated values and formulated maxims are fascinating to a theoretical mind but in actual life they usually prove to be as ambiguous as the oracles of Delphi. True values are only those which emerge during the life of an existing person. The uniqueness of each situation in a person's life will therefore necessarily demand creativity as far as these values are concerned. Acceptance of one man's values and rules by others without regard to their own situations will prove pitifully inadequate. Even the Christian commandment "love your neighbor" is anything but clear in a particular situation. Sartre once used the example of a young man who had to choose between staying home and supporting his aged mother or leaving and joining the French Resistance. Each choice is "good" according to the commandment. What to do?

All existentialists would join in pointing out that in the end every choice made by man is an act of creation, whether we admit it or not. There are those who choose in awareness of their responsibility, freedom, and risk, and there are the others who say they do what norms demand. The latter in order to avoid the actual act of choice will cherish either a minutely detailed ethics with rules for nearly everything or one which allows man to call good whatever pleases him. On the other hand, the existentialist who invents his choices is not quite so anarchic as he may look. First, he chooses fully aware that each act is a decision about his whole life and is irreversible. A responsible choice made in this knowledge will hardly be a reckless one and the act of decision will most certainly be filled with moments of anxiety. Second, as has already been pointed out, even earlier schools of ethics have had elements of invention in their framework. They were merely deemphasized and not talked about. Of course many Christians, for example, rely on their church to spell out in detail what the commandment of love supposedly implies. This is done in the hope of reducing the amount of individual creation needed. But the recurrent controversies over what to do and not to do in each Christian tradition show that such a reduction has its definite limits. Kant's categorical imperative (act so that in each case you know yourself to be a legislator of mankind) is a clear enough challenge to invention. The existentialist, when he today re-emphasizes such elements of a true choice as invention, risk, freedom, and irreversibility is, thus, not at all a latter-day anarchist but a person who reminds his fellow men that in the realm of ethics, as in any other field of philosophy, the existing individual and his action must escape rigid systematization. Even a wonderfully detailed recipe is only a recipe. To make what it describes needs the actions of a cook. And the cook will, despite the most detailed recipe, have to rely on his own decisions and actions, which can lead to quite unexpected results.

Still a few concrete cues concerning the ethical demands of the existentialists can be given. There is first the challenge to overcome one's inertia, present in the temptation not to decide, not to act or at least to follow slavishly suggestions by various agencies of certainty in order to avoid the struggle true decisions require. Second, the challenge to accept one's uniqueness rather than betray it at every moment for the sake of comfort. Related to this, third, is the demand that one fulfill one's potentialities. This may be pictured by Sartre as the ability to transcend oneself constantly, or by Tillich as an essential structure. In every case man is never finished, he is never that which he is at a given moment. Lastly, existentialists have always called for Kierkegaard's inwardness as an important element of ethics, that he must decide and act with a strong sense of personal involvement.

The religious existentialists add another definite demand. Man's actions must aim at a true and living relation to God. Nietzsche's and Sartre's man always stays ultimately directed toward himself. He creates himself in spite of the world and even judges himself. Heidegger's and Jaspers' man aims at something which is beyond himself but in which he at the same time stands. To fail means to forget this standing in Being (Heidegger) or the encompassing (Jaspers). Failure is again judged as a failure by man himself. The religious existentialists resolutely interpret authentic existence as existence in relation to God. Failure (one could also say evil) means to let this relation be disrupted. Tillich would call it continuous estrangement, Marcel failing to bear witness, Buber a variously attempted self-sufficiency or confining oneself to the *I-It* relation, and Berdyaev the betrayal of the meonic freedom man is. Consequently for all four thinkers evil is not a deviation from doctrines, dogmas, and creeds or a breaking of commandments; evil is estrangement of man from what he can be and really is, it is a life of failing to stand in relation to God.

While it still must be admitted that the existentialist emphasis on creativity makes for a lack of concrete rules and directions in the field of ethics, the critics of existentialism have in their ethics neither avoided ambiguities nor achieved that immediacy of challenge to the whole person which existentialism exhibits. The ethics of social approbation, for example, which is so prevalent today, practically smothers individual creativity in favor of passive conformity to whatever society demands. Linked to that is an image of man determined by his environment or heredity and, thus, incapable of any real decision in freedom. Ethics in its true sene is practically abandoned for a science of adjustment which knows no right or wrong but only various degrees of successful adjustment. While such a science of adjustment is detailed enough, one has serious doubts whether this advantage is worth the price paid for it.

2. THE PROBLEM OF THE "OTHER" PERSON

With authentic existence as its central ideal and with its call for the life of the "single one" existentialism has always found the creation of a social philosophy a particular challenge. What does existentialism actually have to say about the problems, ideals, and the resulting relationships of the living together of human beings? An answer to this question is of much more than mere academic import. This is because no era in history has been in greater need of new answers to social problems. Our century has seen wars of unprecedented proportions, revolutions have become almost commonplace occurrences, and the human longing for ideal social justice is being expressed in many ways. But while all of this might have been expected to evoke a clear awareness of the need for new approaches to social problems and for new ideals, too much of Western thought has been content with analyzing and describing existing social situations. Such an approach unwittingly has tended to strengthen one of the great dangers of our era, mass conformity.

Existentialism, of course, never has followed such a course. On the contrary, it has been accused of the opposite danger, namely, that its ideals disrupt the relationships between human beings. Admittedly there have been those among the existentialists who altogether deny the possibility that a lasting bridge can be built from person to person. Kierkegaard—going even further—declares that attempts to devote parts of one's life to the endeavor of establishing a union of some sort with other persons are undesirable (see his attitudes to his own engagement and to marriage). For him man's relation to God absolutely excludes other relations. The "single one" has no other concerns. Sartre, while not questioning the desirability of man's directing his efforts toward a genuine communication with others, says the fulfillment of such attempts is impossible. Sartre's man is encapsuled in his own existence without openings to others. All human relations for Sartre end in failure, since he allows for no true person-to-person encounter. In the course of social relations the "other" is either made an object I try to possess or he makes me the object of his possession. Thus Sartre knows of no partial or total linking of personal destinies. Accordingly "hell is other people" and at the root of all human relations is conflict. But even Sartre, with his radical denial of fulfillment in the social realm, has produced most thought provoking analyses of human relations. Brilliant and keen, they cannot be ignored by anybody really concerned with the true complexity of the social phenomena. This can also be said of Kierkegaard and his work.

Jaspers and Buber stand in stark contrast to this insistence on the intrinsic solitude of authentic existence. They both assert that the authentic person is a "related" person. Jaspers speaks of true communication between *Existenzen* (authentic existences) as an integral part of their constant re-creation. Man is not able to live authentically if he is cut off from others who make the same effort. Buber is even more outspoken when he equates authentic existence with his man of the dialogue between the *I* and the *Thou.* In the view of both philosophers the relation between two persons can go far beyond the mere "staring" at each other suggested in Sartre's work. Relations are possible between human beings which do not impair the freedom or integrity of those communicating. Love and respect can underlie the relations between man and man. All of this is in turn not an unqualified yes to each and every human relation, as it most certainly carries a warning against any social relation which takes in only single aspects of man rather than the whole person.

Between the two positions, the clear no and the outright yes, stands Heidegger. His image of man recognizes both the insistence on human solitude as an essential feature of authentic existence and the emphasis on the *Mitsein* (being with) of others. Heidegger tries to balance the two views and, as usually happens in such a case, has been charged by some with taking a neutral and indecisive position and praised by others for a superb achievement.

Unfortunately the wealth of insights which the probing of the existentialists has developed can never be adequately reflected in a brief summary. Those who know their works will agree that in the keenness of their analysis of the whole complex of inter-human phenomena the existentialists need not be afraid of comparison. In their analysis of human relations they have proved to be the archenemies of all oversimplifications, popular or scientific, and of all stereotypes.

Consequently existentialism dislikes utopias of any kind. (I would view this statement as even being true in Buber's case.) All utopias begin with naive assumptions, such as that man is good but corrupted by external conditions (economic, social, etc.). The existentialists who object to any assertion of an eternally fixed human nature find such a doctrine of the goodness of man to be only one of the more dangerous examples of it. Such innocently naive assumptions have always stood at the beginning of the revolutions which have as their slogan: "After this revolution—the Golden Age." Against all utopias, those glittering temples of perfection, the existentialists put the challenge for every individual continuously to strive for a personal relation with the "other." Abstract schemes, whether pale and merely hopeful simplifications of man's so-called nature or blueprints for the final and ideal organization of society, are just vain expectations. Glittering and promising but not really fitting life, they leave man in the end deeply disillusioned.

A horrible example of this sort of organization are the totalitarian regimes of the twentieth century. They have not been merely the results of dogmatic leaders, or bad economic conditions, as has so often been asserted. Their real source has been the longing of man to find some personality, formula, or aim to which he could abandon himself and, thus, still the craving for a meaning to his life. Modern man, like all his ancestors, wants to feel "at home" in the world. Totalitarian regimes promise easy satisfaction of this craving. Whether under a leader or in a supposedly ideal society, man "knows" that somehow his life has been given a purpose. He need no longer feel alone. The high price of such utopias every contemporary has had and still has to pay. The flight from one's personality and responsibility has proved to be expensive. Against all of these hopes of the ideal and final solution of the social problems the existentialists never cease to put their admonition, "Give up." Utopians are chimeras, and costly ones. To simplify man is easy in the realm of thought. Oppressive coercion is needed, however, to make simplified concepts real. After millions have been sacrificed, the ideal state of affairs still continues to elude man. There is no mere institutional solution to the social problems. The true relation of person to person is an endless task to be accomplished by everyone for himself as long as mankind exists. There are no shortcuts. Even the ideals of a perfect Christian society fall, for nearly all existentialists, into the category of dreams.

Consequently society will have to be organized in such a way that personal communication is facilitated. Although none of the existentialists speaks out directly on this matter, Western democracy has a good deal to recommend itself as that form of social organization, which, if rightly understood, fulfills the demands of the existentialists. First it shares with existentialism the ideal of tolerance. The existentialist admitting that he does not know "the" answer, struggling all the time to achieve a true communication with other existences can hardly be other than humble, and humility in relation to others is tolerance. The demand to be tolerant is, however, only one aspect of the kinship between true democratic ideals and existentialism. Another is the realistic judgment common to most existentialists on the positive and negative influence of the state upon man. They all reject the naive trust in the supposed beneficence of the state which is so popular today. While some social organization is certainly necessary for a civilized life, even for freedom to assert itself, the power given to the state should be carefully examined. The state itself can become a threat to the whole and free person, and this does not exclude the non-totalitarian state. In the period of the mass-media of communication (and thus of mass influence), Nietzsche's warning is doubly timely, namely that the modern state is always ready to develop into a Leviathan.

By far the most important contribution of existentialism to the democratic form of life, however, lies in the rebirth of a true and genuine individualism in existentialist philosophy. Without it the validity of the democratic idea will decrease even in a country whose institutions seem to guarantee eternal life to democracy. For too long much of Western thought has been affirming two contradictory images: on the one hand the democratic form of life has been declared the ideal form of society, while on the other hand the idea of the free and responsible person has been replaced by a concept of man as either naturally or deliberately conditioned by his environment. But democracy dies at the hour the free person is abandoned. And with the exception of personalism no other contemporary school of philosophy can be found which has argued the case of the free personality more convincingly and fervently. Such a free person, an authentic existence, though not the champion of smooth conformity, will nevertheless prove to be the soundest foundation of democratic life.

V. The American Dream and Existentialism

As the journey through existentialist thought comes to an end, the question posed in the beginning concerning the relevance of this philosophy to our contemporary situation returns. All doubts of whether existentialism is a serious enough philosophy to concern oneself about will have long since vanished. What remains is to find the point at which the necessities of our situation are met by the contributions existentialists have to offer.

In this search one encounters sooner or later a basic ingredient of the contemporary situation: the American dream of a world in which a free man lives in a free society. Ever since its adoption as a national goal the problem has been how to understand this mysterious and seemingly bottomless liberty and how to put it into everyday reality. Earlier it was viewed as an innate right and more recently has been seen as a product of the social environment. Over the years our struggle has yielded magnificent achievements in the fields of law, social order, and physical comfort. Paradoxically, despite all of these achievements a mood of crisis has begun to spread. We are besieged by proponents both of simple cures and of inevitable doom, so many of them, indeed, that we have shown signs of weariness about their great profusion. While previous generations have ignored the existentialists in their midst for their own reasons, we may came to neglect existentialism out of boredom. This would be most unfortunate, since the new venture in liberty to come will have to proceed in directions similar to those suggested by existentialist philosophy. Sharing similar directions, they face the same opponents: those who reduce man to a mere composite of rules, functions, drives, or conditioned reflexes; those who declare man to be a plaything of conditions; and those who condone, even promote, the "flight" of man into the faceless mass. In direct opposition to such views, existentialism and the new venture in liberty call for a reaffirmation of the creative and responsible man. Only such a person will be able to fulfill the demands of the dimensions of liberty which have gradually tended to become most generally visible. The period in which liberty could be considered a gift received either at birth or from the social environment has ended. The view of liberty as a comfortable accomplishment which everybody can participate in without necessarily contributing anything to it no longer suffices. What emerges—and existentialist thought has had a major share in bringing it to light—is the most fundamental aspect of liberty, namely that liberty must be worked for by everybody all of the time. Then only does it transcend the level of a tool for a better standard of living and become a life-fulfilling quest. The repercussions of liberty understood in such a dynamic way would be most vigorous.

The new concept of liberty, one could even call it the existentialist concept, brings above all vitality and a constant sense of purpose to the individual life. This is because it implies the need for the constant overcoming of what man is at a given moment in favor of a richer personality; the never ending breaking through to an immediate experience of life; the recurrent struggles against that which has already been formulated, like public opinions, doctrines, and world views; in short never to know the answer before the problem has been experienced; never to be a prisoner to a once-formed self, a routine world, an easy secondhand life. Liberty, thus, becomes linked to uniqueness and creativity on the part of each of us. The free person can only be a creative person, creative in the sense of asserting his uniqueness against all that might destroy it and especially against his own inclination to be indifferent.

In the last analysis, this means that liberty resides as a potential force only in the individual and can not be produced by laws, institutions, or a natural benevolent force. It means further that even in a "free" society only those are free who valiantly strive after freedom while the others are slaves of the greatest of enemies—indifference. The new venture in liberty will then be mainly a battle against human indifference: indifference which seduces us to seek the comfort of the faceless mass, wipes away our uniqueness in thought and action, whispers into our willingly listening ears the praise of such a life, and still makes us believe that we are free just because we happen to live in a particular society. The new view of liberty would hardly make life more restful, but it would certainly be more truly human. Indeed this is the result in which existentialists would be most interested. But it would by no means be the only one. As a genuine upheaval is brought about in the life of the individual man, the various fields of human endeavor would soon show its influences.

Politics, for instance, as that field in which the fateful organization of the power of one man over another is established, would see the death of the concept of the "last great revolution," that which would abolish all wrongs and blaze the trail for the coming of the kingdom of heaven on earth. In its stead would come a highly dynamic concept of justice tied to existing man, his ideas, ambitions, and yearnings. The only never changing element in it will be the presence of free and responsible man.

Another repercussion which can easily be envisaged is that affecting the religious traditions of the West. Here critics of existentialism have placed altogether too much emphasis on what that philosophy might destroy instead of attempting to comprehend a most extraordinary contribution which the new quest for liberty advocated by existentialism can make. It is nothing less than the rediscovery of the radically personal character of the God-man encounter which is at the root of both Judaism and Christianity. After being buried under layers of creeds, dogmas, laws, and theological systems, its unearthing would invigorate the religious life of man more than any other measure and infuse new blood into the body of the religious discussions at a critical juncture of Western history. At the same time a safe distance could be kept from the mere reaffirmation of religious tradition and the pure negativism of naturalistic philosophies.

To these two examples of the impact of the new concept of liberty fostered by existentialism a note of caution must immediately be added, lest even after the preceding study of existentialist thought an utterly wrong impression should be created. While existentialism points out the need for a new search into the possibilities of liberty and even the desirable direction for it, it is not a salvage operation hastily put together in order to recue a supposedly declining Western culture. It desires to speak of and to man and not merely of and to contemporary Western man. When existentialists protest against aspects of contemporary Western life and thought, they do so in the interest of what man could and should be at his best and not merely in order to rectify weaknesses in Western culture. Their pertinence for us derives, thus, not from their will to be benefactors of a specific group of people or age, but from their insistence on always discovering the general human predicament beneath the covers of temporary crises.

Nor do existentialists harbor the faintest hopes that Utopia will be ushered in through the backdoor of existentialist precepts. First, there will always be those who avoid the venture and find comfortable shelter in both the old and the new answer systems. Second, existentialists are keenly aware of how incomplete even man's most perfect strivings are and, with it, of the ever-present possibility of failure. This awareness stems not from any pessimism or melancholy inherent in the personalities of existentialists but from their knowledge of the immense mystery which surrounds the human life. It erects an insurmountable obstacle to the easy hopes of Utopia, whether scientific, religious, or political. It also bans finality in any sense as something man can command. Existentialists have therefore called on man to abandon the ideas of a "final" solution to our practical problems and to our longing for truth. In stead of the ideal of a "final" solution there is the demand to fill our lives with a genuine search and not to be content with pre-formulated answers and past accomplishments. Throughout history, that search alone has evoked the great and the truly humane in man, while of course the situation in which it has been carried on has been changing constantly. Thus, every birth of a human being must signal the beginning of a drama in a unique setting, but with the same obligation to search, to accept responsibility, and to act without any promise that "the great Sphinx will ever speak." A severe prospect, but to avoid this experience is to the existentialist equal to never having been really born.

If finality in the sense of perfect accomplishment is impossible, what about the finality of existentialist philosophy? Existentialists have at no time considered themselves the last prophets of mankind. But the philosophy of the future will never be able to forget their revolt against any philosophy of man which treats him only in special aspects. If nothing else survives of all the existentialists have said, it will be impossible to forget the utter seriousness with which they have dealt with human existence. "I want honesty," Kierkegaard is supposed to have exclaimed shortly before his death. "Truth is courage and error is cowardice," Nietzsche added to this. And in a sense this passionate willingness to search and find and to witness for this supreme personal experiment with one's whole personality is the core of existentialism. It forms the basis for authentic existence, is the key to the overcoming of estrangement, and gives the highest promise for the preservation of free and responsible man.

Notes

I. EXISTENTIALISM AND THE AMERICAN MALAISE

1. Sören Kierkegaard, *Stages On Life's Way* in *A Kierkegaard Anthology*, ed. by Robert Bretall (Princeton: Princeton University Press, 1951), p. 180.
2. *Kierkegaard's Concluding Unscientific Postscript*, translated by David F. Swenson, completed by Walter Lowrie (Princeton: Princeton University Press, 1941), p. 317.

II. EXISTENTIALISM PREPARED

1. *Kierkegaard's Concluding Unscientific Postscript*, p. 182.
2. *Ibid.*, p. 85.
3. Sören Kierkegaard, *The Journals* in *A Kierkegaard Anthology*, p. 14.
4. Sören Kierkegaard, *Attack Upon Christendom* in *A Kierkegaard Anthology*, p. 438.
5. *Ibid.*, p. 447.
6. *Kierkegaard's Concluding Unscientific Postscript*, p. 521.
7. *Ibid.*, p. 49.
8. *Ibid.*, p. 49.
9. For his own study the author used *Friedrich Nietzsche's Werke*, ed. by Walther Linden (Berlin-Leipzig: Deutsches Verlagshaus, 1931). Due to lack of an up-to-date English translation of Nietzsche's works the translations were taken from various sources. For number 9: Preface to *The Will to Power* in *Existentialism*, ed. and with an introduction, prefaces, and new translations by Walter Kaufmann (New York: Meridian Books, 1956), p. 109.
10. *Ibid.*, p. 110.
11. *Ibid.*, p. 105.
12. *Menschliches, Allzumenschliches*, (242), in *Friedrich Nietzsche's Werke*, vol. III, p. 149 (my own translation).
13. *Morgenröte*, (5), *Friedrich Nietzsche's Werke*, vol. IV, p. 6 (my own translation).

14. *Wille zur Macht,* (148), in *Friedrich Nietzsche's Werke,* vol. VII, p. 243 (my own translation).
15. Friedrich Nietzsche, *The Joyful Wisdom,* translated by Thomas Common (New York: Macmillan Co., 1924), p. 152.
16. *Wille zur Macht,* (180), in *Friedrich Nietzsche's Werke,* vol. VII, p. 263 (my own translation).
17. *Untimely Meditation* (*Schopenhauer as Educator*) in *Existentialism,* ed. by Walter Kaufmann, p. 101.
18. Fëdor Dostoevski, *Notes From Underground,* translated by Constance Garnett, as printed in *Existentialism,* ed. by Walter Kaufmann, p. 73. Alternative translation available in *The Best Short Stories of Dostoevski,* translated by David Magarshack (New York: The Modern Library, 1955), p. 133.
19. *Ibid.,* p. 79. (Alternative: Magarshack, p. 293.)
20. Fëdor Dostoevski, *The Brothers Karamazov* (London: William Heinemann Ltd., 1930), pp. 267 f.
21. *Ibid.,* p. 273.
22. Rainer Maria Rilke, *Notebooks of Malte Laurids Brigge* (New York: W. W. Norton Co., 1949), p. 17.
23. Fëdor Dostoevski, *The Brothers Karamazov* (New York: Modern Library, no year) pp. 139 f.
24. Miguel de Unamuno, *The Tragic Sense Of Life* (London: MacMillan Co., 1921), p. 43.
25. *Ibid.,* p. 51.
26. *Ibid.,* p. 107.

III. EXISTENTIALISM ARRIVED

1. Martin Heidegger, Introduction To The Fifth Printing of *What Is Metaphysics?,* as printed in *Existentialism,* ed. by Walter Kaufmann, p. 208.
2. Martin Heidegger, *Sein und Zeit* (Halle, 1927; 6th edition, Tübingen, 1949), p. 34 (my own translation).
3. Jean-Paul Sartre, *Existentialism is a Humanism,* as printed in *Existentialism,* ed. by Walter Kaufmann, pp. 290 f. Alternative translation: Jean-Paul Sartre, *Existentialism,* translated by Bernard Friedmann (New York: Philosophical Library, 1947), p. 18.
4. *Ibid.,* p. 298. (Alternative: Friedmann, p. 34.)
5. *Ibid.,* p. 300. (Alternative: Friedmann, pp. 37 f.)
6. *Ibid.,* p. 291. (Alternative: Friedmann, pp. 18 f.)
7. Karl Jaspers, *Die Geistige Situation der Zeit* (Berlin: Walter de Gruyter & Co., Göschen Sammlung #1000, dritter Abdruck der fünften Auflage, 1953), p. 16 (my own translation). English edition of this book: *Man in the Modern Age* (London: Routledge, 1933).
8. Karl Jaspers, *Einführung in die Philosophie* (München: R. Piper and Co., 1953), p. 28 (my own translation). English edition of this book: *Way to Wisdom* (New Haven: Yale, 1951).

9. Karl Jaspers, *Reason and Existenz* (New York: Noonday Press, 1955), p. 59.
10. Karl Jaspers, *Einführung in die Philosophie*, p. 32 (my own translation).
11. *Ibid.*, p. 43 (my own translation).
12. Karl Jaspers, *Reason and Existenz*, p. 68.
13. Karl Jaspers, *Einführung in die Philosophie*, p. 105 (my own translation).
14. Karl Jaspers, *The Perennial Scope of Philosophy* (New York: Philosophical Library, 1949), p. 105.
15. Paul Tillich, *The Problem of Theological Method*, in *Journal of Religion*, vol. XXVII, no. 1, January 1947, as printed in *Four Existentialist Theologians*. Selected and with an introduction and biographical notes by Will Herberg (Garden City: Doubleday and Co., 1958), p. 250.
16. *Ibid.*, p. 242.
17. *Ibid.*, p. 243.
18. *Ibid.*, p. 253.
19. Paul Tillich, *Systematic Theology* (Chicago: University of Chicago Press, 1951), p. 237.
20. *Ibid.*, p. 240.
21. Paul Tillich, *Biblical Religion and the Search for Ultimate Reality* (Chicago: University of Chicago Press, 1955), p. 51.
22. *Ibid.*, p. 76.
23. II *Corinthians* 5 : 17
24. Paul Tillich, *The New Being* (New York: Charles Scribner's Sons, 1955), p. 19.
25. Gabriel Marcel, *Être et Avoir* (Paris, 1935), p. 243 (my own translation).
26. Martin Buber, *Between Man and Man*, translated by Ronald Gregor Smith (London: Kegan Paul, 1947), p. 184.
27. Martin Buber, *I and Thou*, 2nd ed., translated by Ronald Gregor Smith, (New York: Charles Scribner's Sons, 1958), p. 28.
28. *Ibid.*, p. 4.
29. *Ibid.*, p. 11.
30. *Ibid.*, p. 3.
31. *Ibid.*, p. 4.
32. *Ibid.*, pp. 16 f.
33. *Ibid.*, p. 17.
34. Martin Buber, *Eclipse of God*, translated by Maurice S. Friedmann, et. al. (New York: Harper and Brothers, 1952), p. 123.
35. Martin Buber, *Paths in Utopia*, translated by R. F. C. Hull (New York: Macmillan Co., 1950), Ch. X as printed in *The Writings of Martin Buber*, selected, edited and introduced by Will Herberg (New York: Meridian Books, 1956), p. 126.
36. *Ibid.*, p. 130.
37. *Ibid.*, p. 128.
38. Nicolas Berdyaev, *The Beginning and the End* (New York: Harper and Brothers, 1952), p. 59.

39. *Ibid.*, p. 187.
40. *Ibid.*, pp. 231 f.

IV. EXISTENTIALISM ASSESSED

1. *Kierkegaard's Concluding Unscientific Postscript*, p. 113.
2. *Ibid.*, p. 278.
3. Gotthold E. Lessing, *Werke*, Vol. X, p. 53 as quoted and translated in *A Kierkegaard Anthology*, p. 195.
4. *Kierkegaard's Concluding Unscientific Postscript*, p. 107.
5. *Ibid.*, p. 111.
6. *Ibid.*, p. 111.
7. *Ibid.*, p. 112.

Index